"In this revelatory book, Rev. Wadleigh shares to traveling into our inner darkness with compassion so that we may claim the healing and self-love that lies within."

— HeatherAsh Amara, bestselling author of the Warrior Goddess series

"Shadow work was a key to unlocking the unconscious blocks that were keeping me in so much pain. And Michelle's book is stellar in explaining not only what it is but also how to do it in a friendly and effective way. If you are struggling with moving forward or becoming free in any area of your life, I'm confident there is some shadow there that is calling you to greater healing. This book will not only get you to the shadow—but it will also get you through it and help you incorporate it so you become the master of your inner world instead of afraid of it. All praise to Rev. Michelle for this transformational work."

— Mark Anthony Lord, spiritual leader and author

"With deep love and a gentle touch, Michelle Wadleigh brings to light that which we most want to keep in the shadows and walks us out of the darkness so that we can experience the joy we deserve. Thank you for the gift of this book."

— Rev. Dr. Michele Whittington, author and founder of Unleash Your Life

"You, like me, stand to get the most from this book if you have spent a lifetime hiding from and overcompensating for those aspects of yourself that you've considered ugly, undesirable, and therefore unacceptable. With every chapter, I discovered how self-rejecting I've been and why. By the final page, I was never so glad to be wrong about who I thought I was. I recommend this book with a caution: you, too, may come away feeling dead wrong about who you feared you were and who you deplored you weren't."

— Catherine A. Duca, LCSW and author

"Michelle Wadleigh takes your hand and walks you through a step-by-step process to eliminate blocks, some you didn't even know you had, to open your life to joy."

— Rev. Dr. Wendy Craig-Purcell

SHADOW WORK

ALSO BY MICHELLE WADLEIGH

Forgiveness: A Path, a Promise, a Way of Life

Prosperous Me

40 Days to Freedom: A Lenten Practice for the Modern Mind

SHADOW WORK

A Spiritual Path to Healing and Integration

MICHELLE WADLEIGH

ST. MARTIN'S
ESSENTIALS
NEW YORK

The information in this book is not intended to replace the advice of the reader's own physician or other medical professional. You should consult a medical professional in matters relating to health, especially if you have existing medical conditions, and before starting, stopping, or changing the dose of any medication you are taking. Individual readers are solely responsible for their own health-care decisions. The author and the publisher do not accept responsibility for any adverse effects individuals may claim to experience, whether directly or indirectly, from the information contained in this book.

First published in the United States by St. Martin's Essentials, an imprint of St. Martin's Publishing Group

www.stmartins.com

Designed by Steven Seighman

The Library of Congress Cataloging-in-Publication Data is available upon request.

ISBN 978-1-250-36054-0 (trade paperback)
ISBN 978-1-250-36055-7 (ebook)

Our books may be purchased in bulk for promotional, educational, or business use. Please contact your local bookseller or the Macmillan Corporate and Premium Sales Department at 1-800-221-7945, extension 5442, or by email at MacmillanSpecialMarkets@macmillan.com.

First Edition: 2024

10 9 8 7 6 5 4 3 2 1

To my grandchildren, Lila, William, and Annaliese;
my sons, who keep me tested, Michael, Keith, and Seth,
and their partners, Isis and Julia; my husband, Neil Pinkman;
and my adopted-through-love family, the Gonzales and Reilly families.

Contents

A Special Note from the Author

DEAR READER,

IT WOULD BE UNPROFESSIONAL AND DOWNRIGHT UNCARING NOT TO PROVIDE HERE what might look like a disclaimer but in truth is a loving warning, a reminder of sorts. Shadow work runs deep, can open wounds, and, if not practiced with enough self-care and self-love, could retraumatize you. I bring this work to you from a lifetime of practice inspired by a sheer desire to survive a really hard past. I was blessed to be surrounded by individuals who were also in this powerful and healthy conversation.

Here is what I suggest. First, please move through the material slowly. Also, be prepared to reach for support, whether from a health-care professional or a trusted friend or family member. Keep your support on speed dial—literally. This book is not intended to replace any therapy or medical attention you are undergoing; I am not encouraging you to change your normal routine, or to reduce any medications you might be on. I am asking you to practice radical self-care. The work is deep. It can unearth things that you may want added support to deal with. Consider the book one of your many resources. If you feel overwhelmed at any point, with this or any book you read, stop, take deep and healing breaths, and choose the most positive path to move forward. I care deeply that you do what is right for you. Shadow work can be a part of that journey, to whatever extent makes the most sense to you, and for you.

If you have ever been in a store when a parent suddenly loses sight of one of their curious children, you have heard the panic in their voice as the parent calls out to their child to come back. Imagine if you had that intensity applied to retrieving your disowned parts, the parts of you that have been rejected and projected onto another, causing you, and often the other, great pain and strain.

Imagine yourself finding a painful and rejected part of yourself and instead of indulging in shame, worry, and concern, you try talking to this inner part of you—your inner child, so to speak—and inviting her home, inviting him home, inviting them home. Imagine this process to be loving and safe as I bring this shadow work alive. It will feel safe, loving, and hopeful.

Foreword

IN THE JOURNEY TOWARD SELF-DISCOVERY AND PERSONAL GROWTH, THERE EXISTS A realm often obscured, concealed in the recesses of our subconscious—a realm known as the shadow. Reverend Dr. Michelle Wadleigh, in her profound and illuminating work, *Shadow Work: A Spiritual Path to Healing and Integration*, fearlessly ventures into this territory to guide us through the transformative process of shadow work.

The importance of shadow work cannot be overstated; it is an expedition into the depths of our psyche where we encounter the aspects of ourselves that have long been overlooked or consciously ignored. Michelle Wadleigh masterfully navigates this intricate terrain, seamlessly blending spiritual wisdom, psychological insights, and practical guidance to create a road map for those brave enough to embark on the journey of self-exploration.

What sets this book apart is not only Dr. Wadleigh's deep understanding of the shadow but also her ability to make the profound accessible. Through personal stories that resonate with authenticity and vulnerability, she invites us to see the universal in the particular, recognizing our shared humanity in the midst of individual struggles. It is through these stories that the shadows come to life, offering a mirror for readers to reflect upon their own hidden aspects and uncharted territories.

In addition to weaving narratives that inspire and resonate, Michelle Wadleigh has generously provided a treasure trove of practical exercises that empower readers to engage in their own shadow work. These exercises are not just theoretical concepts; they are tools for personal transformation. From journal prompts to meditation practices, each exercise is designed to catalyze self-discovery and facilitate the integration of the fragmented parts of ourselves.

Shadow Work is more than a guide; it is an invitation to embark on a sacred journey—one that leads to healing, integration, and wholeness. Reverend Michelle Wadleigh beckons us to explore the depths of our being, shining a light on the shadows that, once acknowledged, can become sources of strength and wisdom.

As you turn the pages of this transformative guide, may you find the courage to confront your shadows, the inspiration to embrace your whole self, and the guidance to navigate the path toward a more integrated and authentic life. May this book be a companion on your journey toward self-discovery, offering insights and tools that illuminate the way to a more profound sense of wholeness.

Reverend Soni Cantrell-Smith, D.D.
Spiritual Leader, Centers for Spiritual Living

Introduction to the Concept

TO LET YOU KNOW HOW WE WILL GO THROUGH THIS PROCESS, HERE IS A BRIEF OUTLINE of the journey you are about to take. Think of this as the shadow work map.

There are four distinct sections in this book:

SECTION 1: GETTING STARTED

This section is to inform you about the tools that will be used throughout. It contains information about the creation of your shadow.

SECTION 2: UNDERSTANDING

We will set the stage and provide you with enough understanding to take the mystery out of the work. You will learn a few techniques, but this section is largely to give you ideas and concepts that will help you as you then move into application.

SECTION 3: APPLICATION / DOING THE WORK

In this section you will be guided through the practice of healing the shadow. This is the section where most of the technique and practices are.

SECTION 4: MAINTENANCE

What good is doing this work, only to return to unconscious habits? This section contains tools and tips to stay fresh and present.

Here is the work checklist in order:

1. Do the pre-work.
2. Sign your contract.
3. Set your intention.
4. Establish your why.
5. Do your inventory.
6. Keep the pre-work practices and other suggested practices alive and ongoing.
7. Work the process.
8. Keep maintaining your progress after reading the book.

I bring this work to you not as a psychologist, therapist, or with *any* degree in psychology. While I am a minister and spiritual director, I bring this work to you, instead, from my own personal journey born out of the pain of being *me*. My earliest training was as a hypnotherapist through an organization called the Planned Happiness Institute, so I have come to this path with an understanding of how ideas impact the brain and our consciousness. Once I discovered affirmative prayer as taught by the Centers for Spiritual Living, who teach the Science of Mind worldwide, I recognized immediately that affirmative prayer and hypnosis have the same effect on the brain and in one's consciousness. I now choose to refer to this technique as mindshifting affirmation, but in truth it goes by many names: prayer, affirmative prayer, or spiritual mind treatment.

I am practical, pragmatic, and logical wrapped in a blanket of love, acceptance, and compassion for the hurting heart. This book will be easily readable; the material is easy to ingest and digest. My dream is to influence all individuals to be willing to look at their shadow while maintaining and increasing their self-love.

I do repeat some of the concepts and ideas throughout the book, and I do this on purpose. Sometimes we need to hear (or read) something several times to take it in. Also, repeating it throughout gives you a chance to take that concept deeper each time.

This is a *spiritual* guide through shadow work. I believe that there is only One spiritual power in life, that I call Genius. This One power avails Itself to me at all times in infinite ways. I came to understand that the power of **Mindshifting Affirmative Prayer** is all that I need to transform my life. Now, the use and application of mindshifting affirmative prayer must be properly and potently focused, but once it is, oh, how powerful it is. Let's take a closer look at this.

When you understand how to speak your intentions purposefully and focus your mindful attention on specific areas with emotional intensity, you will then have within your grasp a tool for transformation that is unstoppable. *Mindshifting affirmative prayer seeps into places where nothing else can. Mindshifting affirmative prayer moves whatever is in the way. Prayer opens the space of possibility.* I am going to teach you how to use this powerful tool in your own life.

As I grew in relationship to this power, my faith and conviction grew. As my faith and conviction grew, I was able to feel more and more courageous and ceased the habit of avoiding my emotions.

My emotions are like signposts telling me where to look at myself, reminding me of what needed to be healed and transcended. I have been doing some aspects of this work for more than forty years. I can share with you in all honesty that I am never at the mercy of my emotions. I still have them. I still react at times. I still feel them. But I am no longer afraid. On the contrary: when I catch myself reacting or in judgment of myself or others, I celebrate the experience, because I know without a doubt that I am about to adopt a new aspect of myself since a shadow is showing itself to me, and I will return to an even more complete state of wholeness. You will be able to do this, too.

My desire for you on this journey is that you learn to use your life and its trials and tribulations to identify your shadow, to feel what needs to be felt without shrinking back, to brave the path of wholeness and integration with ease and grace.

So, join me on this journey as we come home to our wholeness with joy in our hearts, curiosity in our minds, and a bounty of self-love. Let's go together, for in community all things are made easier.

SUGGESTION: Find a friend that you trust and feel safe with so you can walk through this together. Having an accountability partner will keep you on task and provide a safe space for you to share as you venture inward. Never try to be their therapist (nor they try to be yours). Hold hands and hearts, but do not try to guide them. Trust their process, and ask them to trust yours. Everyone must move at their own pace, but taking the journey together will help you have support and love while you each do your own work.

Let's be clear.

We each have our own relationship to the power of creation that surrounds us. Your relationship and your name for that relationship in no way hinders the use of this material. Call it what works for you: God/Spirit/Yahweh/Energy/Love/Universal Intelligence/Genius, or whatever else works for you. You can call it your Higher Power, or even just Friend. Just swap out whatever words might distract you for words that work for you. For me, I surrender to an Omnipotent, Omnipresent, and Omniscient essence of good, and I have many names for it. You are free to name and claim your relationship with this powerful universe according to your beliefs. This book can be used by those from any faith tradition, those who consider themselves spiritual-but-not-religious, or even agnostics, who feel there might be "something" larger, but don't have a fixed idea of what that thing is. What you call it isn't important, so please use what feels comfortable for you. You might even find your concept of this Higher Power changing and growing as you go through this material.

I have spent a lifetime learning to identify my parts that needed change and forgiveness. I have also invested thousands upon thousands of hours in silence, meditation, contemplation, and active inquiry to get to know myself and my motivation. These practices helped me crawl out of the hole that I was raised in. My home and my family had a vast number of limitations due to emotional pain, sexual abuse, alcoholism, and a lack of education. Without the principles that I bring to you in this book, my life would look vastly different now.

Please, please be gentle. Please be kind and compassionate toward yourself, and remember to feel good about yourself for choosing to take this journey. Love yourself throughout the book, with each lesson, with each reading.

NEVER EVER LET SOMEONE DISTRACT YOU FROM YOUR SELF.

Why?

Why look at those shadows and face all of those unloved parts in the first place?

- Because trauma and the shadow, represent a complex interplay in the world of psychological and emotional well-being. The shadow contains within it a vast wealth of stored experiences that can undermine us until we come to understand it and develop a relationship with it. It is comprised of the totality of your life experiences and conditioning, yet it is the more difficult things that cause us heartache and unrest. Your deep dive into the shadow is like mining gold: a lot of effort but worth every moment.

- Trauma can hide in your shadow, and if you don't look at it closely and expose it to process and love, the pain of the trauma will remain intact and will affect your life.

- The hidden elements within your shadow, while initially a protective response to the traumatic event, can linger in the subconscious and profoundly influence your thoughts, emotions, and behaviors, even long after the traumatic incident has passed.

The relationship between trauma and shadow becomes a pivotal junction for healing and growth. This courageous journey leads to a gradual release of the emotional and psychological burdens carried as a result of the trauma that lives within our subconscious. It's important to acknowledge that navigating shadow work, especially where your trauma might be involved, can be a sensitive and challenging undertaking, for which the expertise of a qualified therapist or counselor is often needed.

You Do Shadow Work Because . . .

Your shadow contains a wealth of energy, creativity, and qualities that hide within it. It lives at the depth of your subconscious. Each and every time you choose to face a shadow instead of turning away, you position yourself to receive the gifts and blessings that the Universe is constantly trying to show you. But the most important reason is that with each shadow or shadow aspect that you welcome into the wholeness of your being, you become a more authentic, beautiful, powerful, and whole being.

In the midst of each pain you face is a gift, a blessing, so to speak. Each personal challenge sparked by a funky relationship that you seek to understand will leave you more potent to heal this particular relationship and in a better position for all relationships.

Healing the shadow aspects of yourself will also leave you more energized, more hopeful, and willing to engage in life. You will begin to express the creative urge that lives beneath the surface. Serving your "why" will teach you about the hidden blessings in many of life's challenges.

From My Personal Experience . . .

There was a time in my life when I blamed all the bad, all the strain, all the pain of my life on everyone outside of me. I never stopped to consider whether I was responsible for putting something in motion. I was left a judgmental, fault-finding, blaming woman who placed the responsibility of my pain on unsuspecting targets, rather than look back at myself as being the source of the problem.

This left me perpetually a victim, because I avoided owning my part in the discomfort of my world. I was helpless, hopeless, and walked around wearing my victimhood as a badge of honor. After I began facing my own shadows, it became clear that the relentless way I judged individuals was the cause of my relationships not working.

Because I want to support you in clearer understanding, I will offer my own testimony of my personal shadows and mistakes. These stories will demonstrate my past emotional immaturity, my bad decision-making, and how many years I lived at the mercy of my reaction to stimuli from people all around me. I will change some details and names so as not to harm anyone in the telling of my stories.

I will also share stories of students who have walked this path and found freedom. Please note that to protect their privacy, I've changed their names and identifying features—however, the stories are absolutely true. We can learn from one another.

I hope you follow me through this book with a sense of curiosity and compassion. This book will be a complete reflection of spiritual principles combined with solid psychological principles. Using the ideas I write about in this book, I now choose to do all of my work forever from the inside out, from taking responsibility, choosing to apply the aforementioned principles and affirmative prayer, and most definitely choosing to love myself as unconditionally as possible throughout the process.

If you are still reading this—good. Stay, walk with me, love yourself through the transformation while believing in the innate beauty that is your divine birthright. *Shadow Work: A Spiritual Path to Healing and Integration* is a path toward **remembering** who you are, not about becoming something new. We will walk together in love, removing the distractions and blocks while *doing no harm* to ourselves or another.

Thank you for picking up this book, for taking on the task of possibility, and for choosing to return to your WHOLENESS. When any one of us returns to wholeness, the whole of us benefits. Throughout this book, I will provide mind-shift affirmations for you to use along your journey.

Be well, my friend.

Remember to love *all of you!*

Glossary

The Language of the Shadow

USE THIS GLOSSARY TO UNDERSTAND SOME OF THE LANGUAGE THROUGHOUT THE BOOK.

Blessing: To bless is to replace all judgment and condemnation with love and acceptance.

Inquiry: Humans are fascinating beings, and when we inquire within ourselves, we learn about our own motivation. The more we know about ourselves, the better decisions we make.

Law: Law is the term we use to describe the dependable power that acts upon our spoken and unspoken word in order to create. It is dependable as it responds equally to whoever uses this law.

Mindfulness: Mindfulness can take on a few forms. In this book we will encourage readers to become mindful about an aspect of their lives, in other words to expand their awareness of themselves and apply their awareness to choices and behaviors.

Mindshifting Affirmative Prayer: In this book I use the spoken word, which can also be known as affirmative prayer or mindshift. This spoken word is how we use our words to direct our attention to create our desired outcome.

Presence: Presence is the experience of being in this now moment, not concerned about the past or worried about the future. To be present is to be in the moment.

Principle: Principle as it applies in this book is actually referring to the quantum field of creation as scientists have come to understand it. When in the book I say *principle*, I am referring to resting upon the co-creative law of creation.

Radical Honesty: This is the practice of never lying to oneself about what one is feeling, and about recognizing the triggers one experiences that can lead to identifying the shadow.

Shadow: The shadow is the name for rejected parts of yourself that you have projected onto another individual. The shadow remains hidden until we seek to see it.

Sin: In metaphysical traditions like the New Thought movement (which includes the teachings of Science of Mind, Unity, and others), "sin" is often understood as a state of ignorance or mistaken belief rather than a moral failing.

Source: Source is one of many names used to describe the unbridled potential and power that exists at the heart of everything. It is the original cause in the creation of life. Some call it God, Love, Power, Universal Power, etc.

Thought Seed: A thought seed is another term for an idea that has been planted in your consciousness and grows to its intended outcome.

Tissue Issue: Tissue issues are emotions that are still alive today in you that are connected to past trauma.

Getting Started

What Is Shadow Work?

Depending upon what mental health professional you work with or what book you read, shadow work can appear as a highly intellectual and cognitive process, or it can be a spiritual journey through your inner landscape. For me, for us, this book is all about love. Loving yourself enough to do the hard stuff. Loving yourself enough to walk through the emotional baptism by fire. When your love is strong and you plot your way through these emotional waters, navigating the hard stuff, you get stronger and stronger in doing the work.

With *Shadow Work: A Spiritual Path to Healing and Integration*, we heal our shadow through a very loving and accountable process. I will guide you through the application of the tools starting on page 17. The work is about learning to understand the creation of the shadow and then building the muscle and the discipline to stay with it throughout the process. Your job is to be fearless and willing to feel fully all the emotions that will come up, because these emotions contain within them everything you need to transmute those shadows into available pockets of energy.

As a shadow teacher, the most important part of my job is to encourage you not to judge yourselves when you find the hints hidden throughout the work. At times we will identify our own sins (see the glossary, pages 9–10), and other times we will recognize our shadows through our relationships, through our reactions and triggers. And all the while we need to stay loving and compassionate.

Let me be clear here, though: All of the effort is worth it, because you will see the texture of your life change right before your eyes, and you will know that *you* did that. You made the change. You took on the challenge.

> **THE SHADOW REPRESENTS THE DARKER, OFTEN REPRESSED, ASPECTS OF OUR PERSONALITY—THE TRAITS, DESIRES, AND EMOTIONS THAT WE MAY FIND UNCOMFORTABLE OR UNACCEPTABLE.**

Why Is Shadow Work Important?

As you begin to understand the shadow, it will become obvious that you have been trying to arrive at a particular place in your life and just couldn't rise above the trends, patterns, and struggles. Even the glass ceiling that you have been trying to break can be a direct result of your shadow, leaving you scratching your head and wondering why you can't seem to get out of your own way.

As you begin to understand the shadow you will simultaneously see how your life has been impacted by the shadow. You'll find reasoning and understanding in places that once confused you and held you captive. Now, armed with this new knowledge, you will confront the feelings and situations that you previously ran from.

The wide variety of relationships in your life that have challenged you will cease having the power to do so. It will at times seem miraculous, but in truth, it is basic psychology through a spiritual lens. I have witnessed individuals take on integrating their shadow and, as a result, heal relationships that have challenged them for years. Parents who have reunited with their estranged children. Siblings who began to remember that they loved each other. There are individuals who applied the process to relationships with employers and managers with whom they had been struggling, and through the process something magical transpired. Either peace prevailed or they were moved out from under the authority of those difficult personalities.

As you begin to understand that your outer world is a direct reflection of your inner thoughts, beliefs, wounds, and memories—your shadow is comprised of all these—you no longer have to feel hopeless and victimized by life. Doing this work will leave you feeling empowered to heal, rise above, and change the course of those relationships.

Unexamined shadows interrupt our work, our self-expression, our joy, and our relationships. Doing this work is simple but not easy, and yet once you embrace it you get to become a powerhouse of possibility. The work is simple because it is a simple concept. The hard part comes as a result of buying into the belief that your outer world is in charge of your good. To heal is to cease giving power to people and institutions outside of yourself. Every single time that you take ownership of your own experience, you regain more and more of your personal power.

Every time you take responsibility—not blame—you free a part of yourself to be brought home and expressed as joy and as peace. You have everything you need within you to do this. Although we visit responsibility further in the book, let me offer some guidance at this point.

All efforts to place responsibility outside ourselves by blaming another for our situation, reality, or experience weaken our resolve. When you take responsibility, you are in alignment with your personal power; when you blame, you separate yourself from your power. Hence taking responsibility empowers you to move forward.

What Happens When You Don't Do Shadow Work?

Not doing the work leaves you exposed to a boatload of hurt. Not doing shadow work is just shy of not practicing self-care—period. Not doing shadow work leaves you living at the mercy of the conditions of your life. When you don't do the work, you live at the mercy of circumstances and your own reactions to them.

When you don't do the work, you repeat patterns over and over, and wonder why. For example, you marry the same type of person over and over again, or another overbearing boss hires you, or you experience yet another offensive manager at a job that barely pays you enough to live; and then you have to try to survive those unbearable circumstances. Not doing the deep dive might leave you feeling unseen, unloved, and unappreciated. The people all seemed so different on the surface, but you keep having the same outcomes with them.

Until you embrace shadow work fearlessly, you are walking around your life reacting to a variety of stimuli while trying to stay sane and happy. It is not until you are sick and tired of being sick and tired that you will launch yourself face-first into this work.

Shadows appear from a wide variety of situations. Have you ever wondered why you can't seem to get out of a particular loop of reality? Have you wondered why you keep attracting the same crowd of people around you? Have you wondered why life seems so darn hard when you're such a good person inside? Unhealed shadows can also lead to poor health. If you have one diagnosis after another that seems relentless, and you are left wondering why you are always sick, it is likely there are emotional influences involved in your body's struggle.

Without addressing these deep-seated issues, you might find yourself feeling lifeless and trapped, akin to an emotional zombie, devoid of any personal power and helplessly subject to external influences without any obvious way to break free from this debilitating cycle of despair. By learning to interpret the subtle cues from your subconscious, you can distinguish yourself from those who are similarly struggling as you navigate a path toward healing and empowerment.

There is a classic story about faith that's often used to encourage people to accept help. It is about a man whose home was caught in a great flood. He was a faithful man, and when the waters started to rise around his home, he prayed. Soon after he prayed, the emergency services came by to help, but he said to them, "No worries, I prayed—God will save me." As the waters continued to rise, a rowboat came by, and the people in it said to him, "Come in, come in! We'll take you to dry land." And again, he said, "No thank you, I prayed, and God will save me."

The waters continued to rise, and now he was on top of his roof. A helicopter came by and encouraged him to grab the ladder they extended, but once again he said, "No thank you, I prayed, and God will save me." Soon after, the waters covered his home, carried him away, and he drowned. Arriving at the pearly gates, before entering, he asked, "God, why did you forsake me? I prayed, and I was faithful." God responded, "Dear man, I sent you emergency rescue services, a rowboat, and a helicopter; what more did you want?"

The point? There is help and support all around you. You must believe in yourself and your ability to rise up and care for yourself in the most loving way possible, and you must say yes!

How Do You Recognize the Need to Do Shadow Work?

You know you need to do shadow work when you keep dating or marrying the same person over and over again, when you keep working for the same obnoxious boss in all your different jobs, when you react quite abruptly to people you have just met, when you find yourself moving toward or away from people or opportunities without understanding why.

Our shadow is the collection of our past pain, stories, and memories projected out onto the world without understanding. These projections happen quite unconsciously. A hint that work is needed can be anything from large emotional reactions and outbursts or uncontrollable sadness to anger, rage, or depression. Shadows do not look like one specific thing; they have more than one texture.

Remember, shadows can hide in plain sight. These are some of the more obvious signs.

Persistent breakdowns in relationships
Perfectionism and the need to control so you can feel okay
Strong emotional reactions that cause upset, worry, and anxiety
Projection that displays righteous judgment and blaming others
Inner conflict for which you cannot quite put your finger on the source
Low self-esteem

Knowing you have trauma
Difficulty forgiving
Addictive behavior
Depression
Feeling disconnected
Recurring nightmares
Emotional outbursts
Unfaithfulness in your relationships
Being dishonest or tempted to be dishonest

How Is the Work in This Book Different from Other Shadow Work?

First, this work is different because mindshifting affirmative prayers will be used as the healing salve.

Second, this work is different because I do not refer to the shadow as "dark."

Let me explain. We use affirmative prayer or mindshifts to shift our internal view of ourselves, to shift consciousness, and to purge the seeds of conflict that have been living at the level of the subconscious. Direct and conscious application of mindshifting affirmative prayer is the tool that sets this work apart from the other shadow work. Depending upon where you are in your faith journey, you will have to decide how you use this work on the shadow for yourself, and the healing of the shadow through this method. Moving forward, mindshifts will be used to describe this consciousness shifting practice. To make this extremely clear and simple for you to use, this book contains mindshifting affirmative prayer (see the glossary, pages 9–10) in the form of scripts. You can customize these scripts throughout this journey to fit your own unique situation.

If you do not already have experience with using affirmative prayer and its format, you can find step-by-step guidelines in the Maintenance section, at the back of this book. Now, if you have a belief and a practice founded in prayer, the only difference will be my encouragement to use *affirmative language* in a specific way. All affirmative prayer/mindshift is good if you are affirming along the direction of your desired outcome.

Take note that *Shadow Work: A Spiritual Path to Healing and Integration* approaches the healing process from this foundational belief: **There lives within you an innocence, and remembering your innocence is key to doing the work.** In choosing to heal from the effects of the shadow you are already declaring yourself worthy of being free from your own recorded emotional history. How does this history get recorded? It is recorded as an imprint in your consciousness, subconscious, and as trauma in the cells of your body. This work is deep and complicated because as it hides in you, it takes the appearance of normal human qualities. But you were not born to suffer. All suffering and struggling have to be questioned. Without questioning it, it remains our reality.

These scripts are meant to support and guide you gently through this process. The intention of *Shadow Work: A Spiritual Path to Healing and Integration* is to do the work without feeling like you have ripped open a scab and plunged yourself into a state of suffering. We will look at everything with the intention to love *what is* and to accept *what is* as stepping stones to our transformation. We must not fear the pain or feelings that arise; they are the exact fodder needed to reach the plane of existence that we seek to experience.

Every shadow that lives within you has a purpose. The initial rejection of your parts was an effort of your subconscious to save you from some form of pain or discomfort. Your rejected parts are like disowned children who, when invited to come home, get to experience healing and a return to wholeness.

You are about to bring your rejected parts home.

Your Shadow Work Tool Kit

While these might be tools, you can also think of them as gates that you will travel through to reach **Your Whole Self.**

1. Non-judgment
2. Meditation

3. Inquiry and Contemplation and Pondering

4. Affirmation

5. Mindshifting Affirmative Prayer, Also Called Mindshift

6. Blessing

7. Journaling

8. Body Awareness

9. Presence

10. Forgiveness

11. Responsibility, the Power of Ownership

12. Letter Writing

13. Self-Regulation and the Breath

There are a variety of tools to be used and skills to be developed that will make this path a bit easier, smoother, and kinder. I want to make it clear that throughout this journey, priorities of self-compassion, self-tenderness, and self-care are necessary. **These tools must be applied while keeping an open heart and setting an intention for freedom.** At the close of the book, I will return to the tools as I break them down to be used on a daily and weekly basis. Each tool is important, and all are discussed in this book. I also include further resources for some of these topics for you to dive even deeper into.

1. Non-judgment[1]

Practicing non-judgment takes the place of honor as our first and most important spiritual practice. You cannot heal from your shadow if you are simultaneously judging yourself for your behavior, for the shadow as it is projected onto another, or for the mistakes you have made in your life. If you judge yourself too harshly for what you discover about yourself, just like a turtle, you will pull your head in

---

1. This practice is deeply spiritual in its intention and does not mean that any individual should be a victim of, nor condone, anyone's unkindness or cruelty in the name of non-judgment. Sometimes judgment is necessary to survive life. Always practice good self-care and never be a doormat to anyone.

and stop looking. We never want to stop looking, so we begin this entire process by practicing non-judgment.

Humans judge all the time; we are judging beings, and for good reasons (at times). But for our purpose here, we are referring to how we judge to condemn, making ourselves superior and others inferior. We are not talking about the necessary discernment for everyday living. To move through this process, you must accept yourself as you are and as you are not.

HOW DOES THIS SERVE YOU IN RETURNING TO WHOLENESS?
If you cease making yourself or others wrong, you begin to let go and allow truth to be revealed.

2. Meditation

We promote insight meditation, which is the practice of sitting, listening, and allowing yourself to hear and sense the inspiration and intelligence of this Universe. When we are too busy or multitasking or moving from one thing to the next, we can't catch the wisdom that is seeking to be realized.

Meditation works best when you establish one place in your home where you sit every day. Creating this space and habit will act like an ongoing reinforcement, because every time you sit there, your body will instantly begin to plug into Source and synchronize with your own wisdom and intelligence.

If you already meditate, then do what you do already; don't change anything. If you are new to meditation, there are hundreds of videos playing all the right music on YouTube, and there are apps available on your phone. What you don't want is music with a beat or with words. You want to be able to lose yourself in the experience and not get caught up in what you are listening to. Meditation is about listening and receiving, and never about being busy. The simplest form of meditation is to sit, close your eyes, and focus on your breath as you breathe in and out. It is also sometimes helpful to pick a positive word to repeat with each breath, such as *peace*, *love*, *yes*, *free*, or anything else that speaks to you. Explore other forms to find what works best for you.

HOW DOES THIS SERVE YOU IN RETURNING TO WHOLENESS?
Meditation supports you in getting quiet and grounded. There, in that space, you will make better decisions and become more available to connect with your wholeness.

3. Inquiry and Contemplation and Pondering

Socrates said: "To know thyself is to have the keys to the Universe." Inquiry and contemplation might just be the greatest tools of self-transformation there are. Merge the practice of inquiry with the practice of radical honesty, and you will be led to clues of who you are able to be.

Contemplation is about sitting with an idea, a feeling, or a reaction without shrinking back, so you can fully discover what something means to you. In life, things happen, but it is not what happens to us that makes up our lives; it is what we make of what happened, how we hold something inside, and how we speak about what has happened that creates our lives. When we invest enough time looking at our inner landscape, we begin to understand who we are. To practice contemplation, we want to sit quietly in silence for a period long enough to receive the messages of our innermost self.

Pondering is the simple act of watching ourselves and how we react to the world around us. It is lighter than contemplation because it can feel like simple daydreaming.

Inquiry is the action of asking open-ended questions and listening deeply to our inner voice. Contemplation, on the other hand, is the more focused practice of spending time in stillness to understand, witness, and ponder what is before us. You can always write down your thoughts and experiences with this in a journal (see below).

HOW DOES THIS SERVE YOU IN RETURNING TO WHOLENESS?
A practice of contemplation will support you in activating your intuition and inner wisdom that has gone unmined.

4. Affirmation

Affirmation as a term has been overused on every social media platform—so much so that it is often overlooked for the value that it brings to what we do. An affirmation is a simple, short, life-affirming statement that can be easily memorized and used as needed to shift one's attention upward toward hope and possibility.

For example, while doing this shadow work, if you were to feel suddenly confronted by an unexpected and hard feeling, you might have an affirmation at the ready such as: *I am fully capable of facing and navigating this emotion. I am strong.* This is a great example of an affirmation that can be pulled out of your pocket in any moment.

HOW DOES THIS SERVE YOU IN RETURNING TO WHOLENESS?

To affirm oneself is to love oneself. All self-improvement begins with self-approval. Affirming yourself supports this process. We must love ourselves where we are and as we are in order to evolve further into our whole, authentic selves.

5. Mindshifting Affirmative Prayer, Also Called Mindshift

Affirmative prayer or mindshift is the act of speaking a word of affirmation that captures your undivided attention and sets the intention of shifting your mindset. Science has now proven that the body and the mind work together and influence each other. For further investigation into the science, check out *How God Changes Your Brain* by Andrew Newberg, MD, and Mark Waldman. When we speak an affirmation or prayer, our mind and our body are affected simultaneously. Learning to keep your mind and your word synchronized to support life-affirming ideas will support you not only throughout the journey of this book but beyond and throughout your life.

Our world is created out of our words. Our words, fully ingested, will be acted upon not by some superstitious power or deity, but by the universal vibration that creates. Remember, everything is created twice: It's first created in your imagination and then in form or in opportunity, or healing. This regularly spoken word helps you align with your highest and best, preparing you for improved health and happy relationships. And an often-negated perk is that as you raise your understanding and improve the texture of your life, it impacts the world at large—for there is no private good. We are all in this together.

> **HOW DOES THIS SERVE YOU IN RETURNING TO WHOLENESS?**
> The spoken word creates a new inner landscape, one of love, compassion, and acceptance, when used properly.

And, very specifically, when you are able to, speak the words of the affirmative scripts out loud with all of the feeling you can give to them. This makes it easier for you to feel the vibration and power of these words, and shifts are more predictable when we are passionate about what we are saying.

6. Blessing

Let's take this word out of the realm of religion and instead begin to use this word as an action that we take to add love, hope, and renewed possibility to a given situation. Consciously blessing something changes the way we engage with it. For example, if you are someone who doesn't like taking medication, but your body requires that you do, if you bless the medication, your body receives it differently and interacts with it in a way that leads you to greater health experience. A deeper resource for how your body responds to your thinking is *It's the Thought That Counts* by David R. Hamilton. If you are struggling with an individual, blessing them instead of condemning or judging them will alter how you see them.

To bless something or someone is a way of raising your sight as you anticipate a life-affirming outcome. You cannot condemn someone while blessing them. When we condemn, we close down, but when we bless, we open up. Blessing someone or a situation changes the dynamics of what is before you.

HOW DOES THIS SERVE YOU IN RETURNING TO WHOLENESS?
To bless yourself, others, and your shadow is to change the energy around them. Your shadow will reveal itself more easily when blessed.

7. Journaling

Using your journal as a place where you can purge miscellaneous upsetting thoughts, where you can release what has you worried, or where you can say what needs to be said without fear of judgment will support you in freeing stale and stagnant energy.

Journaling throughout shadow work will help you free yourself so you can make room for what's to come. Think of your journal as a place where you can take things like pain or confusion or anger out of your body and onto the page. A journaling practice is great for many things, but specifically it is a very supportive process for shadow work.

HOW DOES THIS SERVE YOU IN RETURNING TO WHOLENESS?
Some of your shadows have lived inside of you for an exceptionally long time. Journaling is a wonderful way to release some of the energy attached to these shadows. In a journal, you are free to express yourself without concern of any judgment or criticism.

8. Body Awareness

Your body is your barometer. Learning to understand the signals from your body will be one of the greatest gifts you give yourself for a lifetime. In shadow work, it is a key that will open you up to the subtle messages that must be acknowledged. Denying the signals of the body—I will say more about these signals a little later—will leave you missing the most obvious clues.

I want to reference two sources to support you here: *Feelings Buried Alive Never Die* by Karol K. Truman, and *The Body Keeps the Score: Brain, Mind, and Body in the Healing of Trauma* by Bessel van der Kolk, MD.

Your body, mind, and heart are tied together. You have all the necessary bells and whistles that you need to get a sense of what is going on behind the scenes. What you need to do is to learn how to read these signals and not try to stop them or change them. They are a gift, a blessing for your wholeness.

HOW DOES THIS SERVE YOU IN RETURNING TO WHOLENESS?

The body is your most dependable biofeedback machine once you learn how to use it and commit to listening to it. Things can get by our mind, our thinking, and we are able to lie (even to ourselves!), but the body never lies. When you are done rationalizing, your body will tell you the truth. This is specifically why numbing your feelings and your body is not a promising idea. To numb your feelings/ emotions is to distance yourself from the clues that your body is trying to tune you into.

9. Presence

Presence is an overused word that is accompanied by a lack of understanding. Presence is the experience of the present moment, the experience of this very moment in time, what is before me, what I am experiencing (even as I read this line). Breathing is an extremely important part of being present. When you are present, you cannot simultaneously worry about the unknown future or be anxious about your mistakes. Presence is now, this moment, this breath, this current experience.

The benefits of practicing presence arise out of untangling yourself from the stories in your head. We don't experience the things that happen to us, we experience what we tell ourselves about what happened to us. Often these stories are filled with your imagination, padded with drama to make it a better story to tell.

HOW DOES THIS SERVE YOU IN RETURNING TO WHOLENESS?
In Western culture we have only been learning about presence in the last few decades, yet learning to be present in the moment is important. To be present to this now moment will support you in detaching from how you have seen yourself, as you allow your new way of being to be fully expressed.

10. Forgiveness

Forgiveness is one of the greatest tools to have in your tool belt throughout this process. There are times when you will see how intricately woven your behavior and decisions are with the emotional pain you are experiencing, which caused your shadow to exist in the first place.

Once you begin to identify your shadow, you will need to have a forgiveness practice in place so you can detach from any personal blame that you might have adopted. This is key to walking the gentle path home. We are not here to practice fault finding; on the contrary, we want to make your journey a gentle and loving one.

The journey that created your shadow was one of inherent discomfort; the last thing we want to do is to exaggerate it. So when you see that a shadow exists due to your decisions, behavior, and judgments, you will want a forgiveness practice at the ready. As you practice forgiveness, you will position yourself to choose self-love, to choose self-tenderness, and to choose self-compassion.

If some of the shadows you identify are the result of abuse of any kind, to any degree, forgiveness is still necessary, but let us be clear here: Forgiveness is never about excusing someone for their behavior. And once again, if you are currently in an abusive situation, please seek help and support. It might not be easy, but you are worth it. You are not meant to be a doormat for anyone.

Forgiveness is about freeing yourself from the pain, which will free you to alter your direction. You free yourself through forgiveness of self and others in order to integrate your shadow aspects back home. Forgiveness cuts the chain of pain between you and the source of your discomfort; forgiveness cuts the cord.

HOW DOES THIS SERVE YOU IN RETURNING TO WHOLENESS?
Forgiveness helps you to break the chain of pain and allows you to be focused on integration without anger and judgment.

I wrote more extensively about this process in my book *Forgiveness: A Path, a Promise, a Way of Life*.

11. Responsibility, the Power of Ownership

Later in the book, I will offer you some additional language and an exercise regarding responsibility, but it is listed and explained here because it is an empowering spiritual practice. You might have heard it this way: Responsibility is the ability to respond. And once you own your reality, you create by choice in your desired direction. No redirection can happen unless you take responsibility. You cannot change something outside of yourself. When you take responsibility, you are working with a shift of attitude, a shift of attention.

HOW DOES THIS SERVE YOU IN RETURNING TO WHOLENESS?
When one takes responsibility, they are empowered to change. It is one of the most important and necessary steps there is.

12. Letter Writing

Throughout the book I will be encouraging you to write letters for different focuses. Letter writing can be a beautiful and creative way to alter how you think and feel about something. It is an important addition to our practices because it will keep you in your heart, and all thorough healing must include the heart.

Letter writing can be done on the computer, but I encourage you to write longhand, and I would even encourage you to use both your dominant and non-dominant hands, because it will keep your thinking fresh. These are not letters to be mailed to others; these are letters for your own healing journey.

If you are a creative, even crafty individual, you might want to create an art journal and add your letters to it. Again, this is you being honest, vulnerable, and creative—a great combination for opening up and healing.

HOW DOES THIS SERVE YOU IN RETURNING TO WHOLENESS?
Letter writing is a beautiful and creative way to shift how you feel about something. As you write a letter, you can pour your heart into it and allow for a shift of perspective to gently take place.

13. Self-Regulation and the Breath

Self-regulation plays a pivotal role in the practice of shadow work. Self-regulation includes monitoring and managing one's emotional responses as one engages with their inner landscape. This includes recognizing and accepting emotions such as anger, jealousy, fear, or sadness that may arise from confronting hidden aspects of oneself. As you learn to sit with your emotions without being overwhelmed or compelled to react to them, you will be empowered to navigate your emotions with greater ease.

Learning to watch and monitor your breath can significantly enhance your ability to regulate your emotions. By focusing on the rhythm and depth of breathing, individuals can effectively calm their nervous system, reduce stress, and create a state of mental clarity and emotional balance. This practice of mindful breathing supports self-regulation, leaving you feeling safe to explore.

HOW DOES THIS SERVE YOU IN RETURNING TO WHOLENESS?
Self-regulation and breathing in shadow work extend to the ability to pace oneself. Since shadow work can be intense and emotionally taxing, it's crucial to know when to delve deeper and when to step back for self-care.

Getting to Know Yourself

Throughout this book, you will be invited to know who you are, what triggers your suffering, and what motivates you toward change. Freedom is the reward for this work. Knowing who you are is the path to retrieve that reward.

Emotional triggers are powerful indicators that can help someone recognize their shadow and identify areas that require exploration and healing in their shadow work.

Here's a list of some of the most common emotional triggers:

CRITICISM: Strong reactions to criticism or feedback, whether it's constructive or not, may point to insecurities or self-esteem issues within your shadow.

ANGER: Intense or irrational anger, especially when it seems disproportionate to the situation, can signal unresolved issues or repressed emotions.

JEALOUSY: Feelings of jealousy or envy often reveal desires, insecurities, or unacknowledged aspects you may want to explore.

GUILT: Persistent feelings of guilt may be tied to past actions or beliefs that conflict with your conscious values.

SHAME: Experiencing deep shame can indicate areas in your shadow where you carry self-judgment or unresolved shame-based experiences.

FEAR: Overwhelming fears or phobias can point to suppressed anxieties and traumas that may be part of your shadow.

INSECURITY: Constant self-doubt or feeling like an impostor can suggest hidden beliefs about your worth or abilities.

OVERREACTIONS: When you react strongly to seemingly minor incidents, it might reveal emotional wounds or sensitivities within your shadow.

PERFECTIONISM: A relentless pursuit of perfection can be an indicator of an unrelenting inner critic or unrealistic expectations.

VICTIM MENTALITY: If you often feel like a victim and blame external factors for your problems, it might indicate a need to explore your own responsibility and power in various situations.

PEOPLE-PLEASING: A tendency to always put others' needs ahead of your own can signify difficulty asserting your own desires and boundaries.

CONTROL ISSUES: A need for control or micromanaging situations may indicate a fear of chaos or a lack of trust in others.

SELF-SABOTAGE: Repeatedly undermining your own success or well-being can point to self-destructive patterns hidden in your shadow.

AVOIDANCE: Persistent avoidance of certain situations or emotions may be a sign of areas you're reluctant to confront.

ATTACHMENT ISSUES: Patterns of unhealthy attachment, such as being overly clingy or pushing people away, can reveal deep-seated fears of abandonment or intimacy.

ADDICTIVE BEHAVIORS: Struggles with addiction or compulsive behaviors often have roots in the shadow, where unmet needs are seeking fulfillment.

EXCESSIVE CRITICISM OF OTHERS: If you find yourself excessively critical of others, it may reflect aspects of yourself that you're not accepting or acknowledging.

These emotional triggers can serve as valuable entry points into your shadow work, guiding you toward deeper self-awareness and personal growth. Recognizing these triggers and exploring the underlying issues with empathy and self-compassion are key aspects of integrating your shadow into your conscious self.

Our job is to follow the triggers of our life—without judgment, recognize they are a sign of our own psyche, take ownership of it, heal it through cognitive recognition, apply the practice of mindfulness, and mindshift so our unwanted parts can come home. Once home, your shadow part will cease needing to project itself onto another, and you can become whole once again.

Understanding

Creation of the Shadow

Understanding how the shadow was created in the first place will be helpful, because when you understand how this process started, you can begin to cultivate compassion for yourself, others, and the pain that accompanies this experience for yourself and the world at large.

The "shadow" is a concept first coined by Swiss psychiatrist Carl Jung in his book *Psychology and Alchemy,* which describes those aspects of the personality that we choose to reject and repress. For one reason or another, we all have parts of ourselves that we don't like—or that we think society won't like—so we push those parts down into our unconscious psyches. It is this collection of repressed aspects of our identity that Jung referred to as our shadow.

Debbie Ford, an expert in the field of shadow work before her passing and author of *The Dark Side of the Light Chasers,* writes: "Our shadow is all the aspects that we reject out of shame, fear, or disapproval. It is made up of any part of ourselves that we believe is unacceptable, will be met with disapproval by others, or that annoys, horrifies, or disgusts us about other people or about ourselves."

You might want to think of your shadow as a cellar where you unconsciously store anything that you do not know what to do with. You're not ready to get rid of it, so you just add it to everything in the cellar. A collection of unnecessary stuff that eventually you will likely just throw out. All those unwanted items have some history and story, but you're not ready to deal with any of it until you have to clear out the cellar to move. You don't want to take everything with you, so you will have to process it when you are moving. This is shadow work: In order to move on, you must commit to processing what has been collected.

Through the creation of these rejected and repressed aspects of ourselves, we begin to distance ourselves from our natural state of perfection and from any aspects that we judge as not okay. These buried personality flaws do not, however, sit innocently within our subconscious.[2] Instead, they sit there festering and growing and interrupting our natural order. Just like an unruly five-year-old, the shadow will get your attention in the most annoying ways. For this reason, shadow work and inner child work are similar. This also leads to the understanding of how our ego is created. Your ego, in an attempt to help you survive painful experiences in your life (such as these rejected parts of yourself), created ways of being that have informed who you are to this day.

These rejected states, just like painful memories, take hold like seeds within your subconscious and, uninterrupted, grow within you, causing you to show up in extremely limiting ways throughout your life. These seeds are not easy to identify, because we project them onto others, and because they become hidden in the first place. In the beginning, we think that others are the problem. In truth, the personality traits that irk you the most in other people are offering gifts of self-knowing for you to embrace. As we take time to love, honor, accept, and forgive the initial cause of these characteristics, we once again return to our wholeness.

It is for this reason that Ernest Holmes, the author of *The Science of Mind*, referred to the aspects of ourselves that we are seeking to heal as *things* that left an imprint upon our consciousness. As our consciousness shifts, so does our ability to free ourselves from this conditioning.

Another way our ego gets created is when we get stuck hiding behind our self-doubts and fears, or whenever we struggle to believe in ourselves. This lack of confidence causes us to hide, and we get stuck. Some of these beliefs are things

---

2. Some further study on buried emotions can be found in the book *Feelings Buried Alive Never Die* by Karol K. Truman.

that we have adopted from outside influences, and others are born of our lack of confidence.

Remember this: The consciousness that existed at the time that you made some of your mistakes or choices does *not* exist now. If it did, you would not be on this journey. Innocence shows itself as we remember that who we *were* is not who we *are* now. Be generous with yourself throughout this process, and be willing to forgive yourself for any errors. Your self-judgment and criticism help to form your shadow.

WHO YOU WERE IS NOT WHO YOU ARE NOW!

The Power of Non-Judgment

"When you judge others, you do not define them, you define yourself."
—EARL NIGHTINGALE

You are going to see a pattern in all this material regarding non-judgment. It is important to practice throughout your processing. It is even important before you begin! In the section of the book titled Application, you will be invited to do three weeks of pre-work beginning with non-judgment.

You cannot proceed if you are feeling defensive, embarrassed, or shameful. All of those emotions are judgments of the self, and they will stand in the way of seeing what shadow is being cast from within. When we judge ourselves, we trip our tendency to defend ourselves; when defending ourselves, we cease being objective in the process. This book and the process require that we move through this process with a light heart. If you are worried about looking good or about the status quo, you will be stuck with what you have. Yes, it is easier said than done, but try this on for size. Make this work playful; look at it as if you are a detective and you are on a journey to uncover the truth. Be willing to laugh at yourself, to bring your hidden treasures (the pain and the shadow) into the light. *Yes, discretion is required here. (If you have some history of harming another and revealing this could reopen the wound for them, please do not. Instead, you will want to work with someone privately to become free of this pain and ensure you are handling it responsibly.)*

PRACTICE: To support your practice of non-judgment, try this. When you find yourself noticing something that you are about to judge, say to yourself, out loud if possible: "It's not good, it's not bad, it just is." Do this regularly and watch how you will begin to soften your view of yourself and others. If this is done rightly and regularly, you will begin to feel more compassionate in general. **Another practice:** When you find yourself judging, simply say to yourself, *Oh, look, I am judging.* If we become the observer, then we can cease judging ourselves for judging and instead just notice the judging.

Learn to pay attention to what you pay attention to, and you will begin to understand your mind and how you created what you are dealing with. For example, if you hear yourself criticizing other parents, you should probably turn and look inward to see how you feel about your own parenting.

If you are criticizing people who are wealthy by using terms like *filthy rich*, you might be projecting your own lack or financial insecurities onto them and criticizing them for making it instead of turning inward to realize your own disappointment.

If you think your husband is lazy or your wife is irresponsible, all these judgments are most likely reflective of some belief you have that may have been born of your family of origin.

As you learn to listen to what comes out of your mouth, if you apply the principles I present in this book, you will learn to read the signs of the evidence that has caused so much of your personal discomfort. You cannot consistently judge and be comfortable. Your judgments weigh you down, and yes, they will lead you to look inside, should you take on that practice, and that is when you will see how much of your life has been created out of this habit.

Over time you will learn to read the signs of your judging. Judgments are a clue to uncovering the shadow, especially when that judgment is accompanied by energy and emotion.

Here are some examples of judgments that serve as hints to your shadow:

- Do you judge people who smoke? The question is: Were you a smoker, or were your parents? As you look, you will see the roots of your judgment.

- Do you judge people whom you perceive to be lazy? Do you question your own ambition or the lack of it?

- Do you walk around accusing others of only thinking of themselves? In truth, are you self-consumed?

- Do you go through life thinking people are arrogant and cocky? If so, where does that behavior live in you?

- Ever meet someone who you think knows everything because they walk around pontificating? Do you have an inner know-it-all?

- Have you ever judged someone for gossiping? Meanwhile, are you gossiping about the gossiper?

Responsibility as a Superpower for Change

When you take responsibility, you reclaim your personal power, but if you blame others or yourself, you are immediately set up for punishment, guilt, and shame. The only true power we have to transcend our pain responds directly to our willingness to take ownership. This power is activated and grows exponentially each time we take responsibility for our lives and experiences. We cannot heal from any pain or suffering until we own it and recognize our responsibility in its creation. I call it a superpower because when we own our experiences and resist blaming others, we will find our inner determination and the strength to change it. When we remain in a blameful, fault-finding habit, we are consistently giving our power away. To remain in your power, you must choose to look at everything in your life both as a reflection of your life and as something that is working for you on your behalf.

This attitude shift from "life is happening *to* me" to "life is happening *for* me and on my behalf" will have you begin to look at all people that you resist in a different way.

I have watched individuals in my shadow classes trying at times to free themselves from the shadow while remaining blameful. This is always a challenge, and it never pays off. When you are doing your work, pay attention when you hear yourself crediting anyone outside of you with the responsibility for your pain and discomfort. Turn this reaction into a red flag that causes you to look back at yourself.

You might be wondering, *how does one who has been abused as a child take responsibility for their experience?* In this case, we encourage you to take responsibility not for the abuse, which no one can condone, but for how you respond to those memories now. You cannot undo what happened, but you can reframe it so it is manageable.

To free oneself from the pain of abuse I suggest this distinction. There is a difference between being a victim and being victimized. Many are victimized—that might be what happened to you—but when you claim yourself to be a victim, two things are happening here.

1. You are identifying with a label that might keep you stuck in pain and suffering.
2. You disempower yourself to find freedom.

We, those who have been abused, cannot undo what happened, but we can cease identifying ourselves in a way that diminishes and causes ongoing pain.

Another aspect of responsibility is accountability. Being accountable is part of taking responsibility. When you become accountable, once again you are increasing your personal power for creating the life you desire.

Now, there is one other part of responsibility that is a tad more complicated. We have already spoken to the fact that we create our world and our reality. In the description of the practices being used within this book, we have stated clearly that you will be encouraged to use the scripts I have provided for your ease, but it is imperative that you understand that your world is created out of your word, spoken or silent. In other words, the thoughts you think, while not spoken aloud, can be as powerful as the words you do speak.

You *create* through this spoken and unspoken word, and you get to decide how to name and identify that power. For some it might be God, for others it is energy, and for others it is all about the quantum field. No one way is right, making the others wrong. We each create our own relationship to the power that exists behind and within all things.

This concept must not be overlooked. You are a walking, thinking, talking, feeling, daydreaming machine. There is no time when all of this internal activity is not in direct communication with the Universe. So, how does this apply to your shadow work? It applies because if you live without growing your awareness of this co-creative process, and instead walk around constantly criticizing yourself or another, what you are actually doing is giving power to those spoken and unspoken words.

Let me tell you a story.

STORY TIME

Meet John, the Unaware Son-in-Law

I had a client, John, who was struggling with his mother-in-law, who seemed to be a quiet, generous, and lovely person by all observations. But he just couldn't let go of the fact that when she would come for an extended visit, she never helped to set the table or clean up afterward. This confused him greatly, because in his family of birth everyone got involved in the meal prep or cleanup.

Often when he was in her company, she lacked warmth toward him, and he didn't understand why, because he never spoke his objections aloud. This is when I pointed out to him the dynamic of how we co-create our world through both the spoken and the *unspoken word*. After chatting about it for a bit, he came to the realization that he was walking around in total judgment of her behavior, and while this was not shared with her in the form of words he said out loud, he was silently communicating how displeased he was with her.

I encouraged him to cease judging her and instead look at where he himself might at times be unhelpful and uninvolved. We spoke again about a month after he took on the practice of personal inquiry and non-judgment. Suddenly the very texture of his relationship to her totally changed, from resentment to loving acceptance, which in turn created changes in his behavior and hers. He realized the connection, but couldn't help but wonder if it was a coincidence, as he was trying to grasp the idea that his internal changes had caused a different external outcome.

Our lives are much more of a reflection of our inner world—I suggest you call it your inner landscape—than one might initially imagine. Simply said, you cannot change what you are not willing to own, so practice radical honesty and name what you see, take responsibility for what is, and then through the practice you will begin to activate the power of change within.

Before we complete this section, let me be clear about why I encourage you to take responsibility as opposed to placing blame. Blame is inherently filled with judgment, accusation, and disowning of the experience you are having. To blame is to hold things outside of you, to push them away. Blaming has a way of relieving you from the feeling of being wrong, because if someone else is wrong it doesn't have to be you.

This feeling, however, is extremely misleading, and if you are honest with yourself, you know what the truth is. You cannot blame another individual and then think that you can identify your shadow and work in the process. Much of my work with individuals leads me to have to constantly encourage them to practice radical honesty with themselves and to take responsibility for what's happened. For many, this is a great struggle. A little hint here: ***When talking about your struggles, if you are constantly using another person's name while doing this shadow work, you are distracting yourself from your freedom.*** You are not clear to heal your shadow until you stop looking at another to blame them for what is (in truth) yours.

Blaming always leads to disempowerment and the draining of your personal energy and power. Listen clearly to your spoken words and to your inner thoughts, and catch yourself as you move to blame another.

 **EXERCISE**

Make a list of the things that you hear yourself blame others for. Most importantly, make sure you are feeling your body while you are doing this. If you pay attention to your body's signals while blaming others, you will likely feel a depletion of your energy.

EXAMPLES: My husband is at fault for our poor communication.
My friend is always late, and I am late whenever I am with her.

_____

_____

_____

_____

_____

_____

_____

_____

Take each statement of blame that you wrote on the above lines and ask yourself this with each person: How much of my energy and personal power am I sacrificing by blaming _____ for _____?

_____

_____

_____

_____

_____
_____
_____
_____
_____
_____
_____
_____
_____
_____
_____

Self-responsibility is key to the freedom that accompanies the practice of identifying the shadow. There are three ways in which we take responsibility, which I will discuss in a bit. This practice requires a lot of strength of character and ownership, and you already possess more of it than you might have realized.

As a personal testimony to the process of taking responsibility for my life through this work and forgiveness work, I have risen to be free of a lifetime of self-judgment and fear. I have personally moved beyond the shame of my family of origin, which included everything from alcoholic parents, to experiencing sexual abuse, to being born into a low-income, uneducated family. I have risen above that and left behind my old perception of myself as a damaged being, as an unworthy, unlovable, invaluable, uneducated, rather stupid woman who lacked vision, creativity, and discipline of mind. Yuck! Growth always comes at the cusp of acknowledging what you believe about yourself with radical honesty and then choosing how to redirect your intention for freedom. That old perception was born out of limited understanding at the time. Those old judgments I made regarding myself have been replaced with compassion and self-love.

But the Genius (my word for God) that is present everywhere, demonstrating as me, kept tugging on my heart and mind, reminding me of who I am and reminding me to plot a course back home. I set my own internal GPS to return to my perfection, and the journey continues today. This book is an opportunity for you to plot a course back to your state of wholeness, a set of directions to return home.

Three Aspects of Taking Responsibility

1. We take responsibility for creating our life and all that is contained within it. **Please do not confuse responsibility with taking blame. If there are aspects of your life that were traumatic, this is not the time to start thinking that the abuse that you sustained was your fault.** Fill out this statement as your commitment:

   Today, (date), I begin to heal from my pain by taking responsibility for the creation of my life. I do so gently, yet earnestly. I remember: To be free from my stories, I must first own them.

2. We take responsibility for how we respond to our life and all that has happened to us and through us. We cultivate the *ability to respond wisely*. This applies even when we feel victimized. We cannot do anything to change what happened in the past, but through taking responsibility for our reactions with non-judgment, learning to identify the shadow will become easier, and we can begin to become strong and free. Fill out this statement as your commitment:

   Today, (date), I take responsibility for slowing down, thinking through, and responding mindfully to my impulses and reactions. I practice non-judgment with myself and others, freeing all from my mind. I am now ready to see how this shadow has been created and am ready to make a difference.

3. As our shadow work begins, we become more mindful and choose to take responsibility for our life going forward by speaking our desired intentions mindfully. Fill out this statement as your commitment:

   Today, (date), I choose to raise my awareness, be mindful of my behavior, and remember that I co-create my world through my thinking and speaking. I stay focused on being renewed and expanded in my understanding. I co-create consciously, mindfully, and powerfully.

There are NO EXCEPTIONS to taking responsibility; however, there is the healing that happens as we take responsibility. *You cannot heal something within that you are not willing to first own.* This is the journey.

Here is an additional practice to cultivate your willingness and make room for more freedom. Let's upgrade some of your beliefs.

🏃 EXERCISE

EXAMPLE: I take responsibility for <u>the kind of mother I was *before I learned better*</u> and free myself to forgive and to be forgiven.

I take responsibility for _____

_____

_____

and free myself to forgive and to be forgiven.

I take responsibility for _____

_____

_____

and free myself to forgive and to be forgiven.

I take responsibility for _____

_____

_____

and free myself to forgive and to be forgiven.

I take responsibility for _____

_____

_____

and free myself to forgive and to be forgiven.

I take responsibility for _____

_____

_____

and free myself to forgive and to be forgiven.

Are you feeling challenged? That is because this is a brand-new way of looking at the pain that remains alive in you. Fear not; it gets easier, and faster. You are more than the pain and the stories. This is just part of the process. A mindshift for accepting responsibility is below.

As always throughout this book I will offer you a mindshifting affirmative statement to pave a new path to your wholeness. Please read all these statements out loud for your best experience.

MINDSHIFT

Taking Responsibility

As I step forward along the path of wholeness, I do so mindfully. Today, as I begin to accept responsibility for the creation and flow of my life now, I do so in the most powerful way possible. This power is the result of being focused and determined to bring home all of my disowned parts.

Taking responsibility for this action empowers me. Yes, I accept responsibility for the creation of or my reaction to the creation of my life. I do this fearlessly because I am focused on my wholeness, and I am willing to walk through this process.

With gratitude, I allow this newly chosen reality to happen now. And I simply allow it to be so, right here and right now.

Imagination and Your Shadow

Because shadow work is a process of exploring and integrating that which is hidden and unconscious, we need different ways to increase our awareness to understand that which dwells within our psyche. Imagination can be a powerful tool in this process as it allows you to delve into your inner world and confront your shadows in a creative and constructive way, while engaging your brain and, of course, your mind-body connection. Using your imagination to see your world in a liberated way can be quite empowering.

Here are five ways to use your imagination in shadow work. It might be helpful to use your journal as you go through each of these:

1. *Visualization of Shadows:* Imagination can help you visualize your inner shadows. You can personify these aspects of yourself, giving them faces, names, and forms. This makes it easier to engage with them, understand them, and work on integrating them into your conscious self. Your imagination can activate untapped resources from within. This will help you develop a relationship with that which is inside of you.

2. *Metaphorical Exploration:* Imaginative metaphors and symbols can help you explore your shadows in a nonthreatening manner. Many teachers use metaphors and archetypes to unearth the truth of the shadow. These scenarios or narratives represent your shadow aspects, and you can use your imagination to interact with them symbolically.

3. *Creative Expression:* Imagination can serve as a channel for creative expression. By using art, writing, music, or other creative outlets, you can externalize and process your shadows. This can help you gain insights

into your inner conflicts and emotions. If you are a poet, write about the shadow; an artist, draw your shadow; a musician, create a song or a chant. Anything you do creatively to engage your shadow empowers you to soften its hold on you and puts you in the driver seat of change and transformation.

4. *Role-playing and Dialogue:* You can use your imagination to engage in role-playing or internal dialogues with your shadow selves. By having conversations with these aspects of yourself, you can gain clarity about their motivations, fears, and desires, which can be crucial for integration.

   Ask your shadow questions like this:

- Shadow, what do you need me to know?
- Shadow, why did you create yourself?
- Shadow, what is the gift you are bringing me?

5. *Future Self-Exploration:* Imagination can help you envision your future self after integrating your shadows. You can visualize the person you want to become. This vision can provide motivation and a clear goal for your shadow work. This positive visualization can serve as a guide for your personal growth. Start by taking a moment to imagine yourself in a dance with your shadow. In the beginning the shadow will lead, but as you stay in your imagination, eventually you take the lead.

Your imagination is a particularly valuable tool in human transformation in general, but very specifically, it is critical to your ability to recreate yourself as you move forward in this work. You want to use your imagination to create a new reality. Imagining yourself as free supports your co-creative process. This is how it works: Because your brain does not know the difference between reality and imagined reality, when you imagine your chosen reality, your brain will react as if what you have imagined is real and send signals and hormones into you to help your process. This is the beauty of conscious daydreaming. We set ourselves on a new path of self-discovery.

Reading Your Shadow Clues

Throughout the book I consistently speak about your emotional reactions, and I encourage you to learn to read your body, because your body never lies. Developing this kind of skill and so many other teachings in the book will benefit you far beyond shadow work. As has been stated before, awareness is curative, but it must have a direction. Awareness alone will not move you closer to your desired outcome. It must be a combination of your awareness and your choice about how to focus that awareness.

This might be one of the most important sections in this entire book, because you have had a lifetime of ignoring your own reactions and body clues by simply disregarding them, justifying them, or distracting yourself by eating, drinking, or turning to other substances.

The world outside of you reflects your inner world. Your inner thinking, your beliefs, and your conditioning collectively make up your worldview. This worldview, if narrow and small, will keep you living at the effect of cause, which means you will be stuck in reactionary responses to all of the world's stimuli. If your worldview gets broader, then you will become more open to innovative ideas and inspirations.

The body you were born into has been conditioned since its conception. Your body has been forming its worldview from the time you were an embryo. Everything that happened to your mother during the time of her pregnancy with you has some level of impact. Science is now definite that as early as eight weeks into creation, an embryo responds to outside stimuli. You have been becoming you since your conception. Your thinking came later.

Your body speaks to you through small and large physical reactions. We would be remiss to honor the larger reactions while ignoring the small, barely perceptible ones, because those small reactions are trying to tell you something; and if ignored over time, those small reactions can turn into larger reactions, with health complications attached. We pay attention to our body as part of the Presence, and we listen with love and curiosity. With love, because this whole book is about being gentle with yourself; curiosity, because curiosity keeps you open to learning about yourself.

Bodily reactions can be displayed in many ways. Here are some examples of ways in which your body has been trying to talk to you:

- Headaches
- Sweaty palms
- Tense muscles
- High blood pressure
- Anxiety and anxious reactions
- Wanting to run from a person/situation: the need to flee
- The impulse to protect oneself: the need to fight
- Suddenly being frozen and not knowing what to say
- Immediate and hard reactions that might display as anger
- Feeling caged or cornered
- Feeling exhausted beyond your understanding
- Struggling to move your bowels: the physical result of holding on for dear life

The above list is an example of some of your body's signs. It demonstrates the various ways in which your body is talking to you, because that is what it is doing. Instead of taking an aspirin to rid yourself of a headache, stop and ask yourself, *What am I feeling, what clue did I miss, what do I need to know?* This type of immediate inquiry will afford you awareness of the situation and the possibility of stopping the headache.

Sometimes our body's messages are quiet and difficult to read or take seriously because they are so subtle and/or we are new to the practice of listening. But paying close attention to those small signals will help you to be proactive and to develop your skill of hearing what your body has to say. The more sensitive you are to these subtleties, the more you can depend upon yourself to pay attention.

When your body reacts, stop what you are doing and ask yourself any or all of these questions: *What's going on? What am I feeling? What clue did I just miss? What do I need to pay attention to?* If this happens when you are around other people, it can be difficult, because you must ignore the temptation to blame another as the cause. If you have any desire to be a masterful spiritual human, then you want to look inside of yourself, not out; you want to take ownership, not give blame; you want to thank the person (shadow) for pointing you back to yourself.

Practice knowing your reactions using the table below:

When I feel angry, I tend to	
If I feel threatened, I usually	
If I feel afraid, I react by	
When I feel excited, it shows by	
When I need to feel comforted, I	

Where I lack confidence, I tend to	
When I feel embarrassed, I	

Rewire Your Brain for Shadow Support

A simple and effective practice for rewiring the brain in the context of shadow work involves journaling, self-reflection, and repetition—*a lot* of repetition. Whatever part of this practice that you learn for the purpose of shadow work will benefit you in many areas of your life. The process will be similar, but the focus can be on anything you choose.

Here's a step-by-step guide to this practice:

1. *Set Aside Dedicated Time:* Find a quiet and comfortable space where you won't be interrupted. Dedicate a specific time each day or week for this practice.
2. *Mindful Breathing:* Begin with a few minutes of mindful breathing to center yourself. Close your eyes, take a few deep breaths, and focus on the sensation of your breath entering and leaving your body.
3. *Reflect on Your Emotions:* Think about an emotion or issue that has been bothering you or causing discomfort. It could be a recurring negative emotion or a specific event that triggers strong feelings. Take a few moments to identify and name this emotion.
4. *Journaling:* Open your journal or a blank document on your computer and start writing freely about the identified emotion or issue. Let your

thoughts flow without judgment. Write about the emotions you're experiencing, the situations that trigger them, and any related memories or patterns you've noticed. Be as honest and detailed as possible.

5. *Challenge Your Beliefs:* After you've written about the emotion or issue, take a step back to review what you've written. Ask yourself if there are any underlying beliefs or assumptions that may be contributing to these feelings. For example, are you projecting your shadow onto others? Are there unexamined fears or past traumas that are at the root of your reactions?

6. *Positive Reframing:* Once you've identified these beliefs, practice positive reframing. Challenge negative or self-limiting thoughts with more constructive and compassionate ones. For instance, if you realize you're projecting your insecurities onto others, reframe this by reminding yourself of your worth and that others may not be judging you as harshly as you think.

7. *Gratitude and Self-Compassion:* End your journaling session by writing down a few things you're grateful for and acknowledging your progress in shadow work. Show self-compassion and remind yourself that growth is a process, and it's okay to have hidden aspects or make mistakes.

8. *Repeat:* Make this journaling practice a regular part of your routine. Over time, it can help you rewire your brain by increasing self-awareness, challenging negative thought patterns, and promoting self-acceptance. Repetition is one of the most important practices needed for any kind of rewiring.

By consistently engaging in this journaling and self-reflection practice, you can gradually rewire your brain to become more aware of your shadow aspects, integrate them, and develop a healthier and more authentic relationship with yourself and others.

MASTERY IS THE REWARD TO THE ONE WHO LOOKS WITHIN, NEVER DISTRACTED BY ANYTHING OUTSIDE.

Reward to Rewire

As you move along through this book doing the work, the easy and the difficult parts, you might at times feel a bit like you are riding on an emotional roller coaster. Once again, it is worth it because, in the end, you will reap the profound benefits of peace, calm, great relationships, health, happiness, love, and freedom. Aren't these benefits worth the path, the feelings, and all the work? I present this to you in the first week of the journey so you can prepare yourself for your own rewards.

In short, we are changing **fear of shadow work** to "I LOVE WORKING THROUGH MY SHADOW. IT FEELS GOOD AND I LOVE MY REWARDS."

Within *Shadow Work: A Spiritual Path to Healing and Integration*, I will continue to remind you to do all your work with a bounty of self-love and patience and without judging yourself for all that you discover about yourself. Moving through this work has left me facing some burning wounds. Each time I ripped off an emotional scab of memories of things I regretted, if it wasn't for staying focused on my reasons for doing this work and the rewards of doing it, I might have stopped the work. (We will visit your "reasons why" in a later chapter.)

But for me, I will walk through the baptism of fire when it means getting to greater freedom. Freedom for what? Freedom to choose the direction my heart and soul desire.

As you do the work, you will definitely benefit from setting up a system of rewards for yourself. It is important that you associate shadow work with a reward. If you wonder why, this has everything to do with rewiring your brain from avoidance of tough work to acceptance of the path that leads to joy, fun, and reward. Rewiring your brain does not happen overnight; it takes an investment of time and attention, and it is not the same for everyone.

I will list some easy and simple suggestions below, but, of course, use your imagination, pay attention to what gives you pleasure, and use your pleasure as a reward for the work you are doing. Rewards should always be of a healthy nature. Try to avoid rewards like alcohol or other substances, or shopping (aka "retail therapy") as a reward. And as always, pay attention to your body's signals. Nervousness will tell you one thing about your reality, but calm tells you something else.

The bottom line here is this: if you *want* to do the work, then establish a reward system to support you in doing the work.

Reward Yourself . . .

- For identifying and facing a shadow head on.
- For each week of work that you complete.
- When you practice forgiveness as part of your shadow work.
- When you demonstrate an obvious increase in non-judgment and curiosity.
- As you recognize that patience and understanding are beginning to replace anger and righteousness.
- Every time you see one of your relationships shifting because of the work that you did.

JOURNAL PROMPT: WHAT WOULD YOU LIKE TO REWARD YOURSELF FOR?
List three to five things to reward yourself for.

_____

_____

_____

_____

_____

Possible Rewards to Consider

- Reward yourself by sitting in a quiet place with a lovely cup of tea or coffee. Try not to use candy, carbs, or alcohol as a reward because you don't want that connection growing in your brain.

- Go for a walk in nature. Nature has a healing quality. Surround yourself with it regularly.

- Call a friend whom you haven't seen in a while and meet for a meal or a walk.

- Create a reward journal, where the sole purpose is to list things that you love, honor, and admire about yourself.

- Create a collage of photos from your past—only things that spark good feelings or photos that are the reflection of goals you have. Add to this collage over a period of time. Remember, every picture you look at needs to spark feelings of joy within you.

- Share your success with trusted friends. Not only is this a wonderful way of being intimate, but you also simultaneously get to celebrate your success and model some good healthy behavior.

- If there is something that you have wanted for some time but couldn't seem to justify the expense of purchasing it, set a reward system up that leads you to finally making the purchase. It is imperative, however, that you set the reward mindfully and responsibly. The last thing you want to do is to seek a reward that creates more stress in your life by causing additional financial strain.

JOURNAL PROMPT: MAKE A LIST OF THE SMALLER REWARDS YOU MIGHT USE DURING THE IN-BETWEEN WEEKS.

_____

_____

_____

_____

_____

_____
_____
_____
_____
_____

Relationships as a Shadow

In relationships, the shadow often emerges when we project our own unacknowledged traits or unresolved issues onto our partners or loved ones. For example, if we struggle with feelings of inadequacy, we may unconsciously project these feelings onto our partner, interpreting their actions or words as judgments or criticisms, even when they are not. This projection can lead to misunderstandings, conflicts, and emotional distance. Moreover, if we suppress our own desires and needs, we may unintentionally expect our partner to fulfill them, placing undue pressure on the relationship. By becoming aware of our shadow and actively working to integrate its elements, we can better understand our own triggers and reactions, which in turn enables us to communicate more effectively, resolve conflicts, and build healthier, more authentic relationships.

Embracing the shadow is not just about self-acceptance but also about fostering empathy and compassion in our relationships. It allows us to recognize the complexities within ourselves and others, making room for a deeper understanding of human nature and a more harmonious connection with those we love. By acknowledging and working on our shadow, we can pave the way for healthier, more resilient, and more fulfilling relationships.

Consistent in my message throughout this book will be my reminder to accept that all of this work is an inside job, and the sooner we take ownership through taking responsibility for our lives, the more empowered we are to create change. While this is true for your chosen journey, it is the breakdown of our relationships that become the signposts, the strain and struggle with family members, friends, neighbors, and especially co-workers. So, while this work is an inside job, you will be directed where to look by reading the signs around you.

Your repressed and rejected parts always get projected onto others—this is the single reason we look at our relationships. Our work is not to change the people in our lives—unless we are unsafe and need to make a healthy decision—or to cast people from our lives, or move away from the troubled people, which is known as a geographic solution. Running from an unworkable relationship will never cure the cause that lives within. Later we will discuss the necessity for self-care and healthy boundaries, which is significantly different from running from our jobs, marriages, and friendships.

If you have a habit of running away from your tough relationships, convinced that they can never be better, or you quit one job because of an idiot boss only to find another job with another idiot boss, you are giving your personal power away. You are actually giving power to people and circumstances outside of you, and this does not work as a permanent solution. While it might provide a temporary sense of relief, it is not long-lasting.

Most people were never trained to look within, to heal and transform. We have been unconsciously reared to think of others as the problem. The news and politics are filled with individuals placing blame outside, assigning fault everywhere. This happens locally and internationally, which is why we as a globe have not found the peace we seek. You know it, you see it, but likely you were hypnotized by a society that doesn't know better. Only now are we finally using words like non-judgment and responsibility at a cultural level. These are concepts that have been taught in the Eastern traditions, but our Western world has been slow to adopt them. Now is the time.

Life is all about relationships. Relationships are our testing ground for how spiritually and emotionally mature we are. Peace cannot be achieved as long as you give responsibility to the people around you. There are exceptions. These exceptions are where abuse and neglect took place, especially when you were a child. Those relationships and the trauma caused by them must be looked at and managed differently and very compassionately. It is imperative that you take responsibility for what is yours, but not for the person you are in a relationship with. There is a fine line that will take some practice to finesse.

Be courageous. Look upon each and every relationship, especially the tough ones, as an opportunity to retrieve an aspect of yourself. The tougher the relationship—meaning the more emotions that you have invested in someone—the greater value that you will receive when the shadow is acknowledged, forgiveness is applied (where appropriate), and full integration of your rejected part back into your wholeness occurs. I have witnessed the miraculous in the lives of individuals where shadow work was applied, and the relationships they once struggled with are transformed. Often it will seem as if the individual you were struggling with changed, but in truth you changed, you reframed the situation, you took responsibility and regained the personal power required to grow into greater wholeness. Our goal is wholeness.

Unless you are living in a cave, you are in a relationship with someone. Even in a cave, away from all people, you are in relationship with your environment. Relationships are where we are most able to recognize our shadows. Listening to the silent or verbal judgments of those individuals you are in a relationship with is your most direct path to identifying your shadow. Noticing your internal reactions and reflections while simply existing inside of your relationships adds depth to your understandings.

If you have ever fallen deeply in love with someone, you know that intoxicating feeling when all is well with the world and all is well with your love interest. In the beginning in love, lustfulness blinds you completely. What happens over time is this: You begin to sober up from your drunken blindness of infatuation and are left engaging your partner, your shadow to their shadow, or any combination of two or more individuals coming together. This also applies in polyamorous relationships.

All that you witnessed growing up in your family created your worldview of how people are in relationship with one another, be it kind and loving, or angry and abusive. If you have not taken the time to heal from early trauma, through therapy or other support, you can rest assured that what was is informing your life today. You and your partners are living in each other's shadows. To approach this work united makes for a powerful working relationship.

Let's state this clearly. When you are in a relationship with someone and that individual has the power to throw you off center either by what they say or by their behavior, there is a shadow. The more reaction you have, the deeper and more painful is the shadow. When you *appear* to not have control over your reaction, this is a definite sign to do some shadow work.

If someone calls you a name or accuses you of some kind of behavior that you immediately object to, you are looking at a shadow. Now, hold on to your hat, *because you are not going to like this one,* but you react to criticism only because some part of you agrees with what was said. Maybe not in your conscious mind, but some part of you agrees to some degree. If I walk up to you and say, "I really hate your purple hair," but your hair is brown, you are probably not going to react, though you might wonder what the heck I am talking about. But if I walk up to you and say, "Man, you really are unconscious and naïve," and that causes a feeling reaction, this would be a clue that you might be feeling unconscious and naïve.

Your reaction is *always* a clue to what you believe within the depth of your being and should not be denied. NO EXCEPTIONS. This is why we speak about body awareness as a spiritual practice. As you raise your sensitivity to your body's awareness, it is important that you pay attention even to subtle reactions. Your shoulders tightening, your stomach feeling like it's in a knot, crossing your arms—any of these might serve as an important clue. Remember—the body never lies; it always provides direct and immediate feedback about the state you are in.

If you react much and often and don't know what to do:

- Say to yourself, "Huh, look at that, look how I reacted, I wonder . . ."
- Keep it light and curious.
- As you replace judgment with curiosity, you begin to free the hold that any shadow has upon you.

- A strong reaction to something said is a clear indication that there is work required.
- A nonchalant, almost absent reaction could indicate that you are free of that commentary.
- Running from a situation is probably the most obvious and impactful sign that you are carrying a wound that must be healed or you will live at the mercy of it forever.
- If you have ever quit a job as a reaction, this is something to take note of.

While we have already spoken about the power of taking responsibility for our lives, I want to make my point again and make it even stronger. Your shadow is yours; it is your creation caused as a result of hundreds, thousands, maybe even millions of different decisions you made throughout your life in an attempt to survive what was going on around you. The people that you react to become part of your creation.

If you and I meet the same person, and you find the person downright annoying and I find that same person interesting, who's right? Is he annoying or interesting? Your opinion does not make this person who they are. Someone's opinion about you does not make you who you are. **What matters here is your perception, your opinion, your labels of the person or situation, and how you react. Your reaction and the feelings that accompany your reaction are the fodder you want to pay attention to and grow from.**

So, while it might look like someone caused something in you, they did not. When someone seems to have power over your emotions, they do not; you are the only one who truly has power over you. They are in your life so you can look back at yourself and call your rejected parts back home. Those seemingly annoying people are angels in your life. Through your relationship with them, you can become whole. You have to see it that way. If you choose to not agree, you will keep this relationship alive in you for years to come and never heal that aspect of your shadow.

 **EXERCISE**

Letter Writing

Let's experiment with shifting perspective through letter writing. I will be suggesting letter writing throughout the chapters of this book. Letter writing is a beautiful and intimate way of shifting perspective.

Before beginning your letter writing, you want to know a couple of pieces of information. They are: what it is about this person that irks you, and what gifts you will receive when this relationship is healed. The purpose of the letter is to create logic that you will depend upon and to make sure you strike a path that is uplifting and supportive.

- Choose a name of someone in your life that you are often irked by.
- Sit down and write them a letter appreciating them for the role they play in your life.
- Thank them for calling your attention to a disowned part of yourself.
- Take responsibility for whatever challenging part of your relationship is your responsibility, and thank yourself for being in this relationship, because without them you couldn't get to this place of your wholeness.

You can also think of this person as a placeholder. What do I mean by that? At an early age something happened that was painful. Your ego developed a coping mechanism, but this coping mechanism often does not satisfy your need to feel okay, and so you judge yourself, reject that part of yourself, and project it onto some unsuspecting individual who appears to have the same characteristics and traits.

They are a placeholder for you, waiting in the shadows for you to reclaim that part of you. Some relationships improve while others end. Not all healing requires us to stay in relationship with the individual we are challenged by. The goal if at all possible is to retrieve our personal power invested in that shadow, heal what's in the way, and leave in a healthy way. If we leave before the healing happens, it will revisit itself upon us. The only exception to this is to leave if you are in any kind of abusive situation. You can work out that shadow in the next relationship. Don't expose yourself to further pain and suffering.

Parenting as a Shadow

What's the matter with kids today? An old line, from an old song, but the attitude is certainly current.

This part of the book and this facet of our shadow work, as it applies to children and parents, is often the least popular conversation that we have. It is filled with triggers for emotions and truthfully, if you are a parent, you might feel tempted to skip over this piece of the work.

Face it, your sometimes annoying, sometimes wonderful, often loving, but also challenging children are reflections of the home they were raised in—your home. Observing our children as a path to our shadow is truly fascinating, although it can be painful. This is not the "old days," where everything was Mom's fault, but it remains true that we are a product of our initial upbringing. Much of who you grew up to be is the product of your experiences with your parents or parental figures, your nuclear family, and your early life experiences, both good and traumatic. There are also your ancestral and cultural influences that are handed down through your DNA.

A bit of my personal experience to offer testimony to this concept. I have three sons. When my first son was born, we were convinced that we had given birth to the next genius or guru. Yes, he was so smart, and beautiful, and spoke so early, he was truly our brilliant son, and everyone agreed. As he grew, some of the shine wore off, and this beautiful, free-spirited boy became a challenge in many ways. I was a young mother, trying to raise a free child but too immature to do so. I was healed enough from the trauma of abuse that I was never cruel in any way, but my lack of parenting skills would begin to shine through. My son is the reflection of my consciousness at the time.

Four years later, almost to the day, I gave birth to another bouncing baby boy. This caused my first son to feel forgotten—I of course didn't forget him in any way, but this was his perception because his world had just changed dramatically. This new son was easier and quieter, but at the age of one, we almost lost him to spinal meningitis. This caused me to stay in the hospital with him as a nursing mom for ten days, leaving my first son to be home missing me and my attention. Son number two was a different child, and because I was a bit more mature and was enjoying an expansion of consciousness, this son reflected the mature me.

Then thirteen years later, while divorcing my husband, I became pregnant with my third son of a different father. I had this son at a much more mature age. I was deeply involved in a spiritual metaphysical community where I was learning all about the concepts that I bring alive in this book. When this son was born, he possessed a deep and grounded calm and a sensitivity to the world around him to the degree that individuals in our community labeled him "the little Buddha." It was a big yoke to bear, so I would ask people not to say that, and I would let him know that he did not have to hug anyone that he didn't want to, so as not to absorb other people's ideas and perceptions of him.

My children each reflected back to me the spiritual and emotional maturity I displayed at the time of having them. And my experience was expressed differently as I matured. I often say that with my first son, "no" meant "yes," with my second son, "no" meant "maybe," but with my third son, "no" meant "no." I believe this happened in large part because of my maturing process.

Every parent wishes they were perfect in their parenting, but no parent is. I look at my children, and they are wonderful, and then again, I look and wonder what mistakes I made, and what I might have done better—definitely fair and sobering questions, but the answers are not always pleasant. Because of my emotional and spiritual journey, I am aware that I did the best I could at the time because of my level of growth and consciousness. As I grew and matured emotionally, I was able to show up better and better. So here I take responsibility for my parenting, but I am also gentle with myself, and I forgive myself for my shortcomings.

Your children reflect who you are. They reflect the parts of yourself that you love and approve of and the parts of you that you don't. This is where we apply some of the spiritual practices within this work. As you do this, practice some radical honesty—not with your children, *only* inside yourself, and remember to feel your body as it reacts to your practicing. This is what the practices applied to this subject would be like:

Take time to contemplate about your child(ren), without judgment and with a sense of curiosity and compassion. _____

_____

_____

_____

_____

What stands out most about your child(ren)? _____

_____

_____

_____

_____

What do you notice about your reactions concerning your child(ren)? _____

_____

_____

_____

_____

Sitting with what has come up, what are some labels that you use to describe the qualities of your child(ren) that most challenge you—in reality, that most annoy you? List the labels here so you can track them. _____

_____

_____

_____

_____

_____

Now, name those qualities and identify the feelings. You have now raised your awareness of what you are dealing with. _____

_____

_____

_____

_____

What are you learning about yourself as you witness your child(ren)? _____

_____

_____

_____

_____

_____

Here is where we ask those necessary three questions (more on the three questions later in the book):

1. Am I those qualities I just wrote down? If yes, the work is here; if not, go on to question two.
2. Have I ever been any of those qualities? If yes, the work is here; if not, go on to question three.
3. Do I judge or object to this behavior/quality/characteristic?

JOURNAL PROMPT: TAKE TIME TO CAPTURE YOUR THOUGHTS AND
REACTIONS BELOW.

_____
_____
_____
_____
_____
_____
_____
_____
_____
_____

Your upset will always be captured within one of those three questions. Now you get to decide how much work you need in this shadow by your level of response or reaction. You might need to just love that inner child of yours that is reflected as your child. You might be called to forgive yourself or another who was part of this creation; or, you can simply bless them and accept the gift of them being in your life and answering that question, helping you become fully healed and integrated into who you are becoming.

Stop looking at your children as anything other than little mini-mes. Yes, if you are divorced and your partner has a challenging personality, they too are part of this creation; it is a shared creation.

When you look at your children, in your mind and heart, think to yourself:

- What do I need to love and accept about myself that is displayed in my children?
- Where have I judged that behavior that exists within me?
- What do I need to forgive about my youthful behavior?

Do all of this inquiry with self-compassion and love.

This inquiry is straightforward, but it will spark some reactions. If you have a child who is majorly problematic, take extra care when making any assessment about them or yourself. Remember—be gentle. This can be a very painful process if your children have deep emotional issues, fears, or behavior problems in school and in the world, but stay with it. The pain can emerge because you will be looking back at your inner child. Don't shrink back from this aspect. But do remember that you are also responsible for raising that independent, tenacious, and hugely confident child. All of their qualities are a reflection of you.

Remember this: Your lineage, good or hard, will be your legacy unless you heal it. You are the change agent, and you get to break the chain of pain as you embrace your shadow and learn to love yourself without conditions. Hurt people hurt people, but healed people *love*. Be the healed individual.

I do want to report to you that all of my inner forgiveness and shadow work have supported me in having wonderful relationships with all three of my sons. The work works if you work it. Taking these steps now—especially before your children have children of their own—will make you grateful in the future.

The reward for seeing your shadow in your children is love, pure unadulterated love. You and your children can grow closer, as you love them without the barrier of your shadow.

AFFIRM: I am willing to see my children as aspects of myself. To love them as they are and to cease placing blame on them for how I feel.

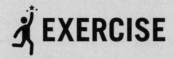 **EXERCISE**

Parent–Child Practice

Before we begin, remember we are dealing with your consciousness, with where your ideas about your children live inside of you, not your actual children. This exercise is always about *you*. Your children are perfect emanations of the Genius that exists. They are on their own journey and, in the words of Kahlil Gibran, "Your children are not your children, they are the sons and daughters of life's longing for itself." You are not doing their work—that is for them to do when they are old enough and ready to do it. You are working on your own shadow, healing your own self. This is for you to do, not to do with or for your children.

Step 1

1. List the most annoying aspects of your children.

_____

_____

_____

_____

_____

2. List the behaviors that irritate you the most.

_____

_____

_____

_____

_____

Step 2

1. Now, begin by first asking yourself, with a single behavior/shadow in mind: Am I that? Have I ever been that? Do I object to this behavior? For example, if you listed "selfish," ask yourself, *Am I selfish? Have I ever been selfish? Do I object to selfishness?* Do this exercise with each characteristic that you have named. Declare this: I proceed with honest, self-revealing answers and look forward to how my relationship with my children matures and grows in love.

   _____

   _____

   _____

   _____

   _____

   _____

   _____

   _____

   _____

   _____

2. When it comes to your children, you need to ask one more important question for each part of this exercise. Ask yourself, ***How do I feel their behavior reflects upon me as their parent?*** Pay close attention to how you answer this question, because it will be one of the more revealing questions to ask yourself when you are willing to be radically honest.

   How does my children's behavior reflect upon me as a parent?

   _____

   _____

   _____

   _____

   _____

_____

_____

_____

_____

_____

If you have followed the exercise as it is laid out, you now know a bit more about what is going on within your parent–child relationship and why. You can begin to see that your children are giving you the gift of loving your unwanted and rejected parts. You and your children can benefit from this: as you begin to love your unwanted parts by bringing those parts home, you will then be able to engage your children as the individuals they are and not only as a reflection of you.

AND TAKE NOTE: Your children are still children, stretching themselves, identifying their power, and seeing what they can get away with. The difference here will be that you can parent from a loving and compassionate place instead of being so emotionally entangled. And when they are at the age to differentiate themselves from you, you will be more prepared to handle their independence. As they grow into the adults they are meant to be, with this work you have done, you will be practiced and ready to handle it when you are not in agreement with their life choices, because there will be those opportunities, more than you might expect. So is the life of a parent. While we love our children, we will not always agree with them. Being emotionally prepared and healing your shadow will set you up for healthier relationships with your children.

JOURNAL PROMPT: IN YOUR JOURNAL, BEGIN TO THANK EACH OF YOUR CHILDREN INDIVIDUALLY FOR THE SPECIFIC ASPECTS YOU ARE LEARNING ABOUT YOURSELF. THANK THEM FOR HELPING YOU TO HEAL AND INCORPORATE YOUR DISOWNED PARTS. USE YOUR REGULAR JOURNAL FOR MORE SPACE DEPENDING ON THE NUMBER OF CHILDREN YOU HAVE.

_____

_____

_____

_____

_____

_____

_____

_____

MINDSHIFT

Shifting Your Parental View

With an open mind and an open heart, I now focus my attention on myself as a parent, and I turn my attention toward my child(ren). I now begin to see where I live in my child(ren) and where my child(ren) live(s) in me. I now cease judging my child(ren) for their behavior or judging myself as a parent. Instead, I look forward to seeing our perfection together as a family. I bless my child(ren) and accept them as a gift in my life. I accept responsibility for my influence over them and forgive myself for any errors.

I love and accept my child(ren) for being exactly who they are and who they are not, and I love and accept myself as the parent that I am and who I wished I were, surrounding all of this in love. I release this word to Universal Intelligence and accept it as so.

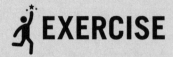

EXERCISE

Letter Writing
Whether your children are still babies or grown adults with children of their own, write each of your children a letter thanking them for their role in your life. Thank them for showing you parts of yourself that you needed to reclaim. In this letter, express your interest in growing in a healthy relationship with your children as adults, in addition to being parent and child. Look forward to learning from each other, loving each other.

Take each of these letters, seal them, and when they are adults or at a time that seems appropriate, take them out and read them, or maybe give them to your children. Pour your heart into these letters; write them to set the intention for being aware and plugged in. This is an exercise to bring healthy and loving understanding.

A Good Time to Remind You

Parenting can be quite challenging and can also be the most rewarding role in life. But it is hard, and you already did and are doing the best you can. Together with this work, you can shift your relationship with your children in the most beautiful and powerful way. This is where the lineage that you adopted can be transformed to a loving and powerful legacy based on truth and healing.

Here is your ultimate goal: to love your children as they are and not as you wish they were, to love them unconditionally even when vastly different from you. This is greatly helped by doing your own shadow work, so you can be more lovingly proactive in your parenting, rather than reactive.

Feelings We Repress, Reject, and Project

The human psyche and our inner landscape form a complex place where the interplay of repressed, rejected, and projected emotions causes our shadows. The impact of these can be profound. When we repress certain thoughts, feelings, or memories, we bury them deep within our subconscious, believing them to be unacceptable or incompatible with our self-image. This is why I encourage you to begin practicing non-judgment at the beginning of your journey, because your judgment of yourself and others is a critical part of creating the shadow.

These repressed aspects can fester, influencing our behaviors and emotions from the shadows. These feelings are so deeply unconscious that our reactions appear to be shocking, but that is only because you have lost track of the root of those painful emotions.

On the other hand, we often reject facets of ourselves that don't align with societal or personal expectations, casting them aside as unwanted. In doing so, we disown these rejected elements, creating a fragmented sense of self, which demonstrates itself through others because we have projected it outside of us. Recognizing and integrating these repressed, rejected, and projected shadow aspects is a vital step in the journey of self-discovery and personal transformation that leads to your wholeness.

For yourself, identify a safe way to express your emotions and spend the pent-up energy caught within them. If you are a parent, help your children to find safe ways to express their feelings, beginning with not shutting them down when they do. Affirm their right to be upset, angry, or scared. If they are young, sit with them through it. If they are older, ask them what they need and ask them if they want you, or if they prefer to be alone. This is a very empowering choice. Then trust them.

Remember it was your denied emotions that got you here, so by doing your shadow work and healing those wounds, you can be a model to your children and others for feeling what needs to be felt and for allowing the process of transformation.

You have come far enough along this journey to understand that the sooner we can become mildly objective about this process, the better off we will be. Our journey is a complicated process of cause and effect.

Shadow Work and Inner Child Work

Some experts would describe shadow and inner child work as being quite different. If this book were of a psychological nature and not spiritual, I might provide definitions to serve that purpose. But for our purpose, we will look at where these two types of work are entangled, where they dance together.

Psychology 101 tells you that you are the product of your early childhood experiences, specifically from birth up to ten years old. These were your formative years, and everything that happened to you during that time of your life has formulated your inner essence and your coping mechanisms.

Your shadow shows up on the outside in many ways: often in work situations or school, definitely in friendships and familial relationships. Your shadows can show up as your hard reactions to something, being immediately angry or outraged, flying off into a jealous spin . . . Once you name the shadow and identify the feeling tone of the associated emotion, you will often be led to early memories. These early memories are of you at a young age, possibly traumatized by what has happened right in front of your eyes. That child, who you will now give an age, is scared, confused, and wants to come home.

It is here that shadow work and inner child work complement each other. This is your opportunity to speak to your younger self who wants to come home, and without this youthful part of you, you are not whole. It might be your curious five-year-old self. Whatever their age, take time to talk to them, to comfort them, and welcome them back home. This tender child ran into something they do not know how to handle, and they need your kindness and care to feel safe enough to remember who they are.

Professionals might choose to distinguish these two aspects differently, but, for our purpose, we will treat them as the same. There will be massive rewards.

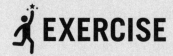 **EXERCISE**

Letter Writing

Write a letter to your inner child. Write it from the most loving and parental place you can write it from. Focus on being the place of love for your inner child.

The purpose of this letter is to:

- See and acknowledge all aspects of your inner child. Let them feel seen and loved. (Presence)

- Thank your inner child for being willing to work with you to heal. (Gratitude)

- Tell them that you love them with all your heart. Communicate your intention for doing this shadow work. (Taking responsibility, love, acceptance)

Whenever you are writing a letter, focus on feeling the shift in your body; stay with the practice until you do feel the shift. Stay with what you are doing until a sense of calm comes over you or until you feel hopeful. These are indications that you have shifted your inner perception.

_____

_____

_____

_____

_____

_____

_____

_____
_____
_____
_____
_____
_____
_____
_____
_____
_____
_____
_____
_____
_____
_____

Hello, Shadow

From the very beginning of this book, I have been encouraging you to be gentle, and to have fun if at all possible. I have begged and cajoled you to not judge yourself for what you discover about yourself, those things that have floated to the surface as you look under all the rocks within your inner landscape. Yes, feelings and memories will surface, but be not afraid—you've got this. You can rise above and free yourself from the shackles of the shadow.

In the nature of keeping this subject light, I want to offer a couple of techniques that you can store away until you need them. These go-to techniques will help you to keep it light and help you to have your heart remain safe and open.

1. *Greet.* Once you start the work and go out in your world and see and/or feel the result of a shadow emotion suddenly rearing its head, just look at

it, feel it, and turn to it and say: **Hello, Shadow, I see you!** I had a student once who, when she started her studies with me, would use this to draw her attention to what was going on.

This technique will be especially healthy if you are around a lot of other people. Imagine that you are out and about when suddenly a strong reaction to someone rises up, but there is no time or place to stop and process. All you do is make the mental note about what is happening by saying, *Oh, hello, Shadow, I see you*. Later when you are home you can process this mental note.

2. *Laugh*. I do not always feel wonderful about or approve of my shadows as they are revealed, but I do trust that I will transcend their gravitational hold on me, so I put it in perspective by laughing at myself and my shadow.

Yes, I am encouraging you to laugh out loud. This is a fantastic way to face the shadow while denying the hold that the associated emotions might have on you at the moment. Once again, we are making a mental note to process it at another time. But the sooner you begin to find some amusement in looking back at yourself, the more empowered you will be. *Laughter doeth good like medicine.* To be able to laugh at yourself while dealing with your shadows will position you to be more objective and less judgmental about yourself.

Combine both techniques to create more impact. Try calling out your shadow with *Hello, Shadow* while looking at the absurdity of your suffering and just laughing out loud.

MINDSHIFT

The Gentle Process of Looking Inward

Today, _____ (date), I, _____ (name), de-clare my readiness and my willingness to no longer live at the mercy of my life circumstances and my reaction to these circumstances. I choose to believe that I am not at the mercy of what was, not now, not ever.

Today, as I begin to engage my shadow, I do so with conscious intent to free myself from all shadows. I believe in my ability to rise above what was and to raise my vibration through conscious intent.

I ready myself to cultivate the faith and conviction of God/Spirit/Life as a healing element in my life.

Yes, I am ready, willing, and able to dance with my shadow, to understand my shadow, and to love myself and be gentle with myself throughout this process.

I surrender my human attachment to my story and to the stain of its pain. Instead, I grab hold of any new beliefs that free me to return to my wholeness and perfection.

During this process, I commit to stop judging myself or anyone whom I have blamed for the current conditions of my life.

I enter this process of transformation with a light and wide-open heart, which allows the Light of the One to enter me and pave the way toward freedom.

I begin my journey now, in love, with love, and with a bounty of gratitude for all who have played a part in my journey. With bountiful gratitude I surrender this word to Love, to Law, and to the Awe of Life.

And so it is.

EXERCISE

Letter Writing

Let's write another letter, this one to your shadow, expressing gratitude while setting the intention to understand and appreciate your shadow for the role it is playing in your life.

Here are a few lines of an example. I offer you this because I am encouraging you to be as loving and kind to yourself as possible. Even if it is not your nature, write it as if it were a love letter to your soul mate.

Dear Shadow,

I want to begin by simply thanking you for all you have done for me by protecting me. I know that was your intention, and for this reason I am eternally grateful. It hasn't always been easy, but knowing that your intention for existing at all is for my good, I am able to let go of judging you. I love you for helping me be me. I do look forward to moving ahead together. With great appreciation, I step away now to go and do my work, learning to love and accept myself as I am and as I am not.

Now, you try. Either on the lines provided or in your personal journal, write a letter with all your heart.

_____

_____

_____

_____

_____

_____

_____

_____

_____

_____

_____

_____

_____

_____

How Self-Love Supports the Process

Self-love and the concept of shadow are two interconnected aspects of personal growth and introspection that play a crucial role in our overall well-being and emotional health. Self-love is the foundation upon which a fulfilling and balanced life is built. It involves accepting and valuing yourself unconditionally, recognizing your worth, and extending compassion to your own imperfections and mistakes. Self-love is not synonymous with arrogance or narcissism but rather a deep and genuine appreciation for your own humanity.

In the journey of self-love, the concept of the shadow, as introduced by Swiss psychiatrist Carl Jung, comes into play. The shadow represents the darker, often repressed, aspects of our personality—the traits, desires, and emotions that we may find uncomfortable or unacceptable. Embracing the shadow means acknowledging and integrating these hidden parts of ourselves. By doing so, we can confront and heal past wounds, enabling us to be more authentic and whole individuals. The process of self-love involves shedding light on the shadow and understanding that it is a part of who we are. By embracing our shadow, we can break free from the patterns of self-judgment and shame, ultimately fostering greater self-acceptance, empathy, and a deeper connection with others. Both self-love and shadow work are integral components of personal growth and inner harmony, guiding us toward a more fulfilling and compassionate life.

Uninterrupted from birth, the love that reared you initially, if sustained and maintained, would grow you into an incredibly expressed and happy human being. This is true for all people; however, there are always exceptions to this rule. As we know, people who feel hurt in turn often hurt other people (as the expression goes, "hurt people hurt people"), but what is also true is that *healed people LOVE*. So, if the love that gave birth to you was never interrupted by life in general, that love would be your complete experience.

Spiritual human beings seeking to be happy and to have a loving and powerful impact upon the world benefit from one focus. What is this one focus? *SELF-LOVE*, to love yourself more, to love yourself as you are and as you are not, to practice self-compassion and self-care. In other words, learn how to raise your self-love quotient. Period. Our suffering is the result of not basking in this love.

Another way to create movement in your life is to focus on your divine perfection, which means the way in which you were designed originally. As you keep your attention there, you will edge out your negative self-talk, which has to be relentlessly monitored. If you believe that you were born in original sin, you might feel challenged by the idea that you were born divinely perfect. I teach, as many metaphysical and spiritual teachers do, that you were born an original blessing, a phrase originally coined by the creation-centered theologian Matthew Fox. This reference says it perfectly. You were born perfect—even when it doesn't feel that way.

Your perfection is not contingent on how you look, where you were born, the color of your skin, or the amount of money you have. You're always perfect in being *you*. Your perfection lives at the center of your heart. It is your untapped potential, and as you move through this work, you will continue to have access to that potential in larger and greater ways.

TO ANY IMPORTANT QUESTION, THE ANSWER IS ALWAYS: *LOVE YOURSELF MORE.*

If you could walk around in the full realization of your Divine birthright and remain in that realization for an extended period of time, the layers of memories, stories, beliefs, and self-judgment that you have gathered through your years would fade into the background and never take root. You might at first think this to be too simplistic, but on the contrary, let the idea fill you and you will be moved. A practice and commitment to loving, accepting, and honoring the self will grow you in unexpected ways. Your self-love and self-judgment cannot coexist.

You thought that the suffering and the limitations were more real than your beauty and perfection. You weren't taught to honor yourself. Your shadow exists because it was given room and power. But you are not your limitations, you are the fullness of your being. Period. You need to retrain your attention.

Your job is to raise:

- Your self-love
- Your self-acceptance
- Your self-esteem: All self-improvement starts with
    ○ Your self-confidence and self-approval
    ○ Your self-worth
    ○ Your self-care

How do you raise yourself up? Doing your shadow work is part of it, practicing forgiveness is another aspect, and turning your attention toward appreciating your beauty and perfection *as you are* with the support of letter writing and speaking aloud mindshift affirmations will help you get there.

Below is a list of ways to begin raising your self-love quotient.

- Start a gratitude practice for who you are. List your qualities and accomplishments nightly in a journal and read them again in the morning.
- If you make a mistake, forgive yourself—IMMEDIATELY.
- LAUGH OUT LOUD at yourself.
- Affirm, affirm, affirm yourself.

- Never speak a word against yourself again—ever.
- Never criticize yourself.
- Face your mistakes honestly but with tenderness.
- Stop all complaining.
- Practice wonderful loving self-care.
- Practice kindness with yourself and others.
- Look in the mirror as you declare: I love you!

STORY TIME

A Story about Judgment and Tenderness: Rev. Sandy

I have a friend who is a minister. She was a dedicated, hardworking minister for a spiritual community, but while she was serving her community and the world, she was fraught with an inner voice of self-judgment and self-criticism that was all-consuming. Her inner judge was strong, and it was having its way with her. She shared with me that she spent a lot of time twisting herself into a pretzel in order to get the approval and support of her leadership and congregation. It was a struggle that she would remain aware of and be at the mercy of for many years.

The way this showed up was with congregants constantly criticizing her in a gossipy way, consistently offering negative feedback about her, and saying that she didn't spend enough time with the members. She felt like she was being watched and judged all the time. This feedback landed with great intensity because she was running around working hard to earn acceptance and approval. You see, she was trying to make the grade by attempting to fix things outside of her. Remember when we don't take ownership and we are distracted by the outer world, we are always left disempowered and unable to change.

Sandy found her way into my shadow class, and once she settled into the aspect of responsibility of the creation of the shadow, Sandy came to realize that all of the criticism and negative feedback she was receiving was a direct reflection of what she believed about herself. All of these incidents reflected her self-doubt and lack of self-worth. She identified with her younger self between the ages of eight and ten years and saw how painfully insecure she was. It all felt the same. Her eight-year-old self and her current self were dealing with the same emotions.

As she healed, Sandy practiced some wonderful tenderness and began to share all she learned. Everyone around her benefited, and all of the negative feedback ceased.

I, too, discovered early in my life that it is all too easy to over-criticize myself. As a mother, my sense of responsibility for my sons blinded me from having an objective look at them. I was too busy feeling at fault. I did have some self-awareness at the time, but shadow work came much later. I remember the habit of horrifically beating up on myself for all of my large and small transgressions. I did not have any patience with my own growth and had little compassion for my parenting. For me, before shadow work, mothering was painful.

Not only did I lack any self-tenderness, but I was downright abusive to myself. The pain of my self-abuse had long-standing impact. The ways in which we abuse ourselves can be quite subtle and toxic. To practice self-tenderness, we must be disciplined to see ourselves through the eyes of love every single day. Anyone to ever look at a brand-new baby, kitten, or puppy has thought to themselves, *Oh my, how precious, what a perfect little being.* I ask you this: When did you stop deserving to be loved in this manner?

Raising your self-love quotient in addition to your self-acceptance, self-esteem, and self-confidence is the only path to truly opening your heart and to loving yourself through this process. You need to love yourself enough to walk this path fearlessly, even when it gets tough.

The following is a mindshift affirmation script to support your efforts, but let's be clear about why self-love matters before we move on. When you are busy loving yourself, you cease judging and blaming yourself, you develop self-compassion and acceptance, and as you look at the world through that worldview, you will be more willing to identify your shadow and to welcome it home with love. The initial projection will cease to exist.

To love yourself is to love and accept all that is the way it is, shadows and all.

The following is a mindshift script for raising your self-love.

MINDSHIFT

Today I Raise My Self-Love Quotient

It is with conscious intent that on this day, I choose to focus my attention on all that is good, holy, and sacred within me. I begin to recall and remember that I am a child of the Beloved One and as Its offspring, it is natural and normal for me to experience myself as worthy of all of my Divine Birth Grace.

Yes, I love myself now as I am and as I am not more than ever before in my life. I accept myself exactly as I am and as I am not. I accept me as the spiritual human being that I am with all of my interesting characteristics and foibles, for they are all good and all part of my being.

I begin to admire aspects of my being that I have not paid attention to until now and value all of it, all aspects, all expressions, all of how I show up. With every moment that I invest in myself, my self-esteem and self-confidence grow in extraordinary ways. Yes, I am here to be expressed as whole, perfect, and complete. As this transformation takes hold within me, my sense of self and my natural self-worth increase, and they do so without my having to prove myself in any way.

The self in me that matters is the Self that exists everywhere. Oh, what a glorious and amazing thing it is to be in the presence of Love as me. This is my truth now and forevermore, unfolding and increasing in expression.

So, gratefully I release this word and allow it to be so and to be my truth.

And so, I let it be.

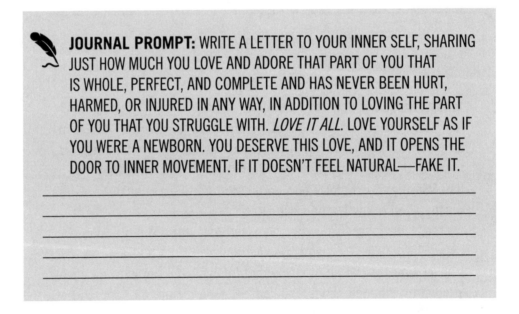

JOURNAL PROMPT: WRITE A LETTER TO YOUR INNER SELF, SHARING JUST HOW MUCH YOU LOVE AND ADORE THAT PART OF YOU THAT IS WHOLE, PERFECT, AND COMPLETE AND HAS NEVER BEEN HURT, HARMED, OR INJURED IN ANY WAY, IN ADDITION TO LOVING THE PART OF YOU THAT YOU STRUGGLE WITH. *LOVE IT ALL.* LOVE YOURSELF AS IF YOU WERE A NEWBORN. YOU DESERVE THIS LOVE, AND IT OPENS THE DOOR TO INNER MOVEMENT. IF IT DOESN'T FEEL NATURAL—FAKE IT.

Being Present

Being present is a fundamental aspect of shadow work, as it enables individuals to engage with their innermost selves and navigate the often complex and uncomfortable terrain of their subconscious. When we are fully present, we become acutely aware of our thoughts, emotions, and bodily sensations in the here and now. This heightened awareness provides a solid foundation for exploring our shadow, which encompasses the hidden aspects of our personality, such as suppressed emotions, fears, and unresolved conflicts.

In the context of shadow work, being present allows us to observe our thoughts and feelings without judgment. By staying in the present moment, we can objectively examine our reactions and triggers, which often originate from the shadow. This self-awareness is essential for recognizing patterns and understanding how our past experiences and repressed emotions influence our current behavior and relationships. Additionally, being present helps us cultivate self-compassion, as we learn to accept these darker aspects of ourselves without condemnation.

Furthermore, the practice of mindfulness and presence can serve as a powerful tool for uncovering and integrating the shadow. By staying in the present moment, we can tap into the depth of our inner selves and gradually bring to light the hidden aspects that have been affecting our thoughts and actions. This process allows us to work through unresolved issues, heal emotional wounds, and ultimately become more authentic and whole individuals. In essence, being present is the gateway to the self-awareness and self-acceptance necessary for successful shadow work, paving the way for personal growth, inner harmony, and more authentic relationships.

Practicing presence is spoken about by yogis, meditation and spiritual teachers, and mystics worldwide. It has been used as a spiritual practice for as long as spiritual teachers have existed. Our human experiences of fear, doubt, and worry stand contrary to presence and exist in the past and in the future, but cannot exist in this current moment. Fears stem from a wide variety of unknown sources. Because you are *not* in touch with your ability to take full responsibility for creating your world, fear of what's to come blinds you and often keeps you paralyzed.

Doubt is the result of you not being in touch with your power. You have a belief in being less than, in being at the mercy of being separated from Source. You doubt yourself because you have not learned to believe in yourself with full confidence as the co-creator that you are.

Worry is a misuse of the law, the law of creation or manifestation. Worry is the fastest way to create what you do not want, because worry has emotions attached to it. If you have any understanding of creation, you already know that a clear idea attached to an emotion generates a result. So worry plus feeling equals a result for what you do not want.

Try replacing worry with statements of affirmation. This is a much better use of your time and energy when thinking about a loved one.

BEING A WORRYWART.	BEING POSITIVE AND LIFE-AFFIRMING.
I am so worried about Uncle Frank and his drinking.	I know that he can find peace. I see him as whole.
I am so worried about my diagnosis.	I rest in faith, trusting that all is working out for me on my behalf.
My son/daughter just got their driver's license.	Every time they leave the house with the car, I stop and say a little prayer of protection.

Your shadow is not now, *it is not a present experience,* it was born out of your past, your experiences, your emotions, and out of your ego trying to support you in surviving whatever was the current experience. We know this already from earlier in this book.

This is a logical progression. If you can get to and maintain a sense of presence (being in this moment), there is no room for the shadow. Practicing presence will help you to take a respite during your day to create this open space of nothingness. When we say nothingness here, we mean not dragging what *was* into this *now* moment. When you can clear that mental/emotional space of what *was,* moments of pure inspiration and joy show up right where you are.

Here are some practices to stay present.

Meditation and deep contemplation are terrific ways to slow down to hear your inner voice. All forms of meditation are helpful, and *there are plenty of apps* to help you start if you are not already a meditator, or you can go to YouTube and search for meditations for beginners.

Throughout your day, get grounded by looking around and asking yourself, *How am I right now, what am I thinking and feeling, where is my attention?* Do this throughout the day and call your own attention back to your present moment.

When a reaction begins to surface, ask yourself this: *Is there anything for me to do about this right now?* If yes, do it. If not, release yourself from the stress of fixing the situation, knowing that when you're ready for it (as long as you keep practicing) the answer will come.

Crucial point here. At no point am I saying that self-reflection will not be painful at times. But the pain is *always* temporary and is a necessary part of your journey, like a stepping stone to your transformed self, to remember who you are. Healing your pain now is better than continuing to be affected by it in the future. Freedom is the reward for all this work. And, if you begin to look at your past, which is what this work is all about, with a prevailing lightness, you can become more objective in witnessing yourself.

Understanding Spiritual Bypass

"It doesn't matter how spiritually developed we are if we remain ignorant of our shadow, staying blind to our less-than-noble motivations for getting spiritual, unaware of how what's unhealthy or immature in us shows up in—and often is masked by—our spirituality. All too often, spirituality is a flight from shadow, an attempt to escape what we're keeping in the dark. Such spirituality is little more than avoidance in holy robes, wherein dissociation masquerades as transcendence."

—Robert Augustus Masters

It is good to understand the meaning of spiritual bypass and all its implications to the work that we are doing here. Spiritual bypass means to use spiritual principles to avoid dealing with reality, feelings, or experiences. Spirituality is meant to go deeper, but spiritual bypass means to use spiritual ideas or terms to avoid going deeper. It is avoiding something uncomfortable under the guise of spirituality, rather than dealing with it directly.

Spiritual bypassing can lead to a superficial sense of peace or enlightenment that is built on a shaky foundation, potentially resulting in the reemergence of those suppressed emotions and issues later on.

Recognizing spiritual bypass while refraining from practicing it allows us to cultivate a more holistic and integrated spiritual and personal development journey. It encourages self-awareness and self-compassion, where we acknowledge that spiritual growth includes embracing our humanness, with all its flaws and imperfections. By facing our shadows and working through our challenges, we can achieve a more genuine, lasting sense of well-being and self-realization, grounded in authenticity rather than avoidance.

Many times we humans are not truth tellers, and this is for many reasons, including our addiction to being liked and to being nice so we can get approved of. There is nothing more inauthentic than someone denying their reality and subjugating themselves to receive conditional love and approval. When a behavior becomes so socially acceptable, even when it is false, it also becomes the norm and sets expectations that have been applied but not consciously agreed to. So I am saying that lying for good reasons is accepted as normal.

The kind of lying I am speaking of right now is more about lying by omission. This is what happens when you want to be a highly evolved spiritual human, or highly successful, or seen as an expert on a subject, and when you can't measure up, you alter the truths or exaggerate or straight out lie. This happens when someone asks you how you are, and you answer, "Fine," when the truth might be otherwise. We either lie not to upset the individual we are speaking to, or we lie because we are feeling a level of shame.

When we deny our reality and customize who we are for approval, this action is a fast track to creating and feeding your shadow.

A shadow cannot live in the open. When in the open, exposed to light, love, and truth, the shadow will begin to dissolve, and you will be able to see it for what it represents within you. As you can see, practicing spiritual bypass can be harmful to your emotional health.

Thinking Versus Feeling

To think and to feel are two completely different things. Both are necessary when it comes to the balance of life, but they carry unique qualities. I have worked with hundreds upon hundreds of people one-on-one, and hands down one of the greatest challenges they have after feeling the pain and shame of discovering their shadow is the ability to identify what it is that they are feeling.

Learning to name and identify your emotions is a key component to raising your emotional intelligence quotient. There are a number of reasons that we avoid even trying to identify our emotions. Not only is this subject important enough to analyze as a vital part of your shadow work, but it's also an important part of getting to know yourself. As Socrates stated: "To know thyself is to have the keys to the universe." Once you have the ability to name "that" feeling, you will be many steps closer to finding your inner path to wholeness. Your feelings will lead you to your memories, which will help you offer love to your shadow fragments.

This is a list of reasons that we might choose to distance ourselves from our feelings. I offer you this list, but in no way should you see it as a block. You have the power not to be stuck by these emotions. You are more than what you are feeling.

Here are some obstacles that get in the way of identifying feelings/emotions:

1. *A lack of emotional awareness.* It is possible you were not reared in a household that had healthy emotional language and awareness. Have hope; this skill can be developed.

2. *Being fearful of vulnerability.* Many individuals believe that remaining guarded and unavailable keeps them safe. Not only is this not true, not being vulnerable can cause a load of additional challenges, and being unavailable to love is at the top of that list. When we choose not be to vulnerable, we are also unavailable to our good and love that might be waiting in the shadow.

3. *Repressed emotions and judgments.* Repressed emotions live at the very heart of shadow work; clearly, they are a cause. We repress emotions when we have first judged them as unclean, shameful, or unsafe.

4. *Lacking clarity.* Although every emotion/feeling we have has a particular identifying texture, there are nuances regarding some emotions that can make it a bit difficult to differentiate one from another. People often confuse jealousy with envy, sadness with grief, or guilt with shame as a few examples. The differences might appear subtle, but when you are looking for clarity, understanding their nuances becomes an important task.

5. *Guilt and shame.* I want to highlight these two emotions because of their direct impact upon shadow work. I like to use Brené Brown's distinction of these two emotions. It is simple and clear. *Guilt is when we have done something wrong, shame is when we are wrong.* When work commences, old memories about our bad decisions and actions arise and, if we are feeling shameful, we will stop looking. Guilt, on the other hand, might serve you in choosing to change a behavior, rightly used, we can alter some of our habits. Understanding the difference and being able to recognize the experience within you will help you decide what there is for you to learn from these two distinct emotions.

6. *Culture.* There is one overlooked reason that we encounter when it comes to labeling and understanding our emotions, and that is the culture you were born into. Some cultures are loud. They connect loudly, they debate loudly, and they love the same way—aloud and very demonstrative. But for some, the display of emotions is rude and uncouth. This can lead to judging the expression of emotions by another, which can be an indicator of a shadow in the one judging.

7. *Avoidance as a trauma response.* There are millions of people who were reared in an unsafe home, a place that should have been safe, but instead was the source of trauma, leaving one to feel fearful, untrusting, and wanting to simply push away the associated feelings. Avoidance provides space, but it also leaves a gap between our repressed emotions and our ability to face them and integrate them.

8. *Name that feeling.* Another bit of guidance from Brené Brown in her book *Atlas of the Heart*: Brown encourages us to expand our actual language for emotions, giving us the tools to communicate clearly to another what we are feeling. This is expressly important if you are a parent or teacher. We must influence those under our care to use clearer language so we can communicate more clearly.

9. *Not making shadow work a priority.* For many, especially in the speedy Western world, we are moving around so fast, working to make ends meet—who has time to think about the shadow? Some people are so consumed by the busyness of their life that they don't stop to know that suffering is not required.

10. *Denial and spiritual bypass.* When one is really unequipped with dealing with emotions, denying them is often a first attempt at being okay. Either we deny them, we justify them, or we turn them into a story. We're willing to do anything but face them head on. Avoidance can be deadly, and when you avoid your emotions completely over the long term, the energy generated by those unexpressed emotions can cause serious health problems.

Application / Doing the Work

We have looked at what the shadow is and how we can interact with it. Now, let us launch into shadow work with a mindshift affirmation.

MINDSHIFT

Beginning the Journey

I open my heart as I begin this journey. I have chosen to do this work in concert with the material within this book, and yet I take full responsibility for making this choice, which empowers me even more. I move forward feeling empowered, ready, and willing to face what I need to face in order to find the freedom and the healing that has been held captive within my shadow.

I choose now to move forward in love and with love on this adventure. I am ready to practice radical honesty, to put the spiritual practices in place to give myself the time necessary to meet my own requirements to complete this work. I anticipate more freedom and I anticipate loving and accepting myself more than I ever have before in my life. I trust myself. I trust this process. And I bask in the sweet reward that this work brings me. With a bounty of gratitude I release this word to be fully demonstrated.

TAKE NOTE: You could be tempted to go to the application before reading the other material in the book. I would strongly recommend that you do not. The world doesn't need you to be a follower, which means doing something automatically. Growing one's awareness opens doors to understanding and readies you for the application. Gather the information and understanding first, and you will feel more empowered. And although this was originally created to be a short six-week program, in reality, the six weeks is the amount of time it will take for you to grasp the concepts, but you will be doing this practice for a lifetime. I recommend taking your time and digging in.

I AM WORTHY OF DOING THE WORK AND REAPING THE REWARDS.

Step One: Pre-work

You picked up this book either intuitively or at the suggestion of a friend or therapist. That's a great start, but as both the author and a teacher, I have learned over these many years that new thinking habits are not the easiest to adopt. I strongly encourage you to commit no less than one solid week (but ideally three to four weeks) to the pre-work before doing the direct shadow work. As a teacher it is my intention to share with you specific skills but also support you in developing new habits for a lifetime.

This deep interpersonal work is a lifelong journey that can be described in three parts.

Part one—Pre-work: This is the point where you make the decision to do the work, gather your resources, and get the support or materials.

Part two—The work: Once you have the information, now you have to apply what you have learned and do the deep work.

Part three—Maintenance: The third is the forever part. This part is critical because it is where you acknowledge that you must be diligent over your mind, your heart, and your awareness. As you age and mature, the maintenance becomes most valuable.

The intention of the pre-work is to help you raise your awareness, to help you learn how to **pay attention to what you are paying attention to**. You have a shadow because your ego has been trying to protect you your whole life, but some of the thinking habits that this has left in you are working against you now. Thorough and permanent change requires a clear new direction and repetition. To rewire the brain we must change our minds and keep them changed until the shift becomes our new habits. This work is as important as all the suggested spiritual practices.

Think of pre-work as stretching before you go for a run; warm muscles react much better than cold muscles. Well, this pre-work will teach you so much about how you use your mind, you will be shocked. Oh, the lessons you are about to learn. I'm happy for you because a new aware mind is a beautiful thing to behold.

There are four parts to the pre-work. You can use them in any combination. You can practice them all together or take on one at a time. If you are new to interpersonal work, I would say go slowly—you know the old adage, crawl before you walk, walk before you run. Welcome to the world of self-awareness, a powerful place to be.

The parts are:

- Practicing non-judgment
- Practicing non-complaining
- Practicing non-gossip
- Tracking your emotions

For at least one week, but ideally three to four weeks before moving to the application side of this book, commit to the pre-work. Remember that to heal a shadow is good, but to gain self-awareness so you can continue to make plans for the rest of your life is the ultimate.

Here is my suggestion for a plan.

1. Choose a start date. Then start the pre-work with non-judgment. For our purposes, we will keep this simple because there are so many nuances within this practice. Primarily, you are on the lookout for spontaneous judgments. The goal is to learn how to watch your mind. This might sound odd, but most people do not have any clue about the nature of their thinking or that their thinking causes their focus, and that their focus attracts all the things that make up their lives.

   Today, (date), I commit to the practice of non-judgment. I commit to not judging myself or others.

   Humans evolved as judging beings for survival. Judging another was how we decided if we were safe of not. And in our modern day form we still make judgment calls all day long. What you are looking to do is to watch what, why, and who you judge. Do you judge from your own insecurities? Do you judge to make someone inferior and to feel superior? For more information look on page 33. Do this for at least one week.

YOU CARRY THE WEIGHT OF YOUR JUDGMENTS WITHIN. YOU CAN NEVER BE FREE OF THEIR IMPACT.

2. Closely related to non-judgment is non-complaining. The difference between them is that you can judge all day long in your own mind, but once you begin to verbalize your judgments, they become a complaint. Complaining and judging are toxic habits. The complaining hurts the complainer more than anyone else because you are carrying it inside.

Today, (date), I commit to the practice of non-complaining and any closely related habits like blaming or fault-finding.

I'm certain you can recognize the logic of practicing both non-judgment and non-complaining simultaneously. This pre-work is about teaching you lessons about yourself for a lifetime.

So, start with both non-judgment and non-complaining together, or practice this one on its own for the second week. You choose; this is your journey.

3. Non-gossip as part of our next pre-work is likely the most difficult for most people. It is often difficult because it is the most quietly socially acceptable and toxic habit there is. I have extensive explanations for this work, but for our purpose here, we will keep it straightforward. Approximately thirty years ago, after reading Don Miguel Ruiz's book *The Four Agreements*, I went on a serious journey of applying the agreements because my life was a mess. I was so moved by the changes I was making that a partner and I created a workshop to bring the agreements alive.

Today, (date), I commit to the practice of non-gossip and enjoy the freedom of being in integrity.

Practicing non-gossip changed my relationships and my sense of self forever. It was the first time that I got to understand how much my behavior had been creating my relationships and why people didn't trust me. I was a total and complete gossip. My mother spoke two languages, complaining and gossiping, and so I learned them well. I was living at the mercy of these habits without understanding the impact upon myself and the people that I care about.

Learning to watch my mind, choosing to not gossip, complain, or judge laid a path for my freedom, the freedom I continue to enjoy and expand upon. Once again, you can do all three things together or you can schedule them separately.

4. Track your emotions. Tracking your emotions can be complicated, so be gentle with yourself, especially if you are someone who has difficulty identifying your emotions and your feelings. God bless intellectuals and academics—they are a wonderful grounding element for our society and for progress, but some of these very same people have great difficulty knowing their own emotions. Unfortunately, this is a cornerstone of all interpersonal work. Whether you are reading this book because someone suggested it to you or because you were drawn to it, you are required to *feel*. To feel is to know you are alive. And to transform, you will need to know what is running you, what emotions are running your life.

Here is what you do—should you accept this life transforming assignment:

🏃 EXERCISE

1. Buy yourself a small notebook or journal, but make sure that it is something you can keep with you for the entire week that I am suggesting you practice this.

2. Throughout your day, set an alarm on your phone to go off every hour. The moment it rings ask yourself: *What am I feeling right now?* And track your answers in that notebook. Do not judge your feelings, and do not judge yourself if you are unsure. Be patient and compassionate with yourself; remember, all self-improvement requires self-approval, and you can't experience self-approval if you are judging and shaming yourself.

3. After a week of tracking your emotions, look over your lists and notice trends and patterns. What emotions did you find yourself

tracking more than others? List them below so you can keep an eye on them while doing the other work.

_____

_____

_____

_____

_____

_____

_____

_____

_____

4. Now look back at this experience and check in with yourself: How are you feeling about what you are feeling? Have you judged yourself or were you kind? Are you disappointed or feeling relieved? Take note and journal on the lines below.

_____

_____

_____

_____

_____

_____

_____

_____

_____

This practice can be done in concert with the other practices or alone. Only you know for sure just how much expansion of awareness you can handle.

IMPORTANT NOTE: DON'T GO FORWARD WITHOUT THE PRE-WORK. Your life is about to change forever, so give it its due attention with all the effort you can summon within you.

Step Two: Set Your Intention (Your Desired Outcome)

On the lines provided, write down what it is that you care to receive from this book even before you begin the work. Be generous with yourself. By *generous* I mean reach high, reach for your dreams of wildly and wonderfully expressing the true, authentic you. Your freedom will depend upon the intention you set. The greater the intention, the greater the gift. Also, if it is too easy to accomplish and your hands are not sweating just a bit, you haven't reached far enough.

It is through setting an intention that we direct the flow and the outcome of our lives. Intentions are powerful and will always help you in acquiring your desires. Intentions draw the best possible outcome from a situation. It is about setting up your own expectations that drive your focus. Without intentions we are like a rudderless boat. Intention, attention, and focus push you toward your desired outcome.

Set your intention:

Example: My intention is to completely free myself from any shadows that impact my emotional freedom. I seek to live a life of freedom and joy.

On the lines provided, write down what it is that you care to receive out of this program even before you begin the work. Be generous with yourself. Your freedom will depend upon the intention you set. _____

_____

_____

_____

_____

_____

_____

Contract

Please read these words very carefully. Before signing, make sure you understand what you are getting yourself into. Stay vigilant while being gentle. You, your whole you, are worth the work.

> *I agree to venture into this life-altering and affirming practice in the most gentle and loving way possible. I agree to love myself throughout this process, to remember that I was born in a state of perfection and my process is simply a return to this state. I remember who I am and who I am meant to be.*
>
> *I agree to cease judging myself, my reactions, my emotions, and my past. I am here to remember my innocence and to be whole again.*
>
> *Sign* _____
>
> *Date* _____

Establish Your "Why"

Understanding your highest motivation for *why* you do anything will keep you in touch with your values. When your passion and your why are synchronized, you can move mountains.

KNOWING YOUR WHY WILL KEEP YOU MOTIVATED TO KEEP ON KEEPING ON.

Asking *why* is an important, transformational question! Your why uncovers your motivation.

WHY GO THROUGH THE PAIN OF THIS PROCESS? WHY DELVE INTO YOUR PSYCHE? WHY BRING UP OLD FEELINGS? WHY BE BACK IN PAIN?
We cannot transform what is inside unless we are willing to feel the pain. Note: If you are at risk of re-traumatizing yourself, slow down, get support, and come back at a later date. You do *not* want to re-traumatize yourself.

This is why we begin here . . . A strong why will help you to stay focused on the desired outcome when it gets hard. Individuals who have journeyed before you have healed their illnesses, established meaningful relationships, and have freed themselves to live extraordinary lives as fully expressed, creative, and successful individuals because they set their sights on their intention and their why. I have personally witnessed movement in these brave individuals who, through the process of ownership, found true peace, happiness, and freedom.

To support the process, you will have to learn how to identify what is going on inside of you. For some people, this is easy; they live with their hearts on their sleeves. No one has to guess what they are feeling or reacting to. This can be a cultural thing; some people are very physical and heartfelt while others are more staid and reserved. For those who are less in touch with their emotions, their investigation into the self will have to begin by observing their reactions and working backward, by noticing their choices and by looking at how others respond to them. A slightly different direction but just as effective.

One way to excavate the shadow is to begin with what you want to avoid, what easily upsets you, or what could easily get you up on a soapbox.

These questions will help you recall what you are moving away from:

- What pains or irritates you over and over again?
- What patterns do you notice?
- What personality types do you always run into?
- What patterns, themes, and trends are in your life?

- What do you hate?
- What angers you easily?
- What triggers unconscious responses?
- What do you feel righteous about?
- What do you fear and have feared for a long time?
- What are your common complaints about people?
- What type of person, or groups of people, do you run from?

What is your why? Where do you want to go?

Have your journal handy to use throughout this process.

Arrange to have some quiet time, sit down, read the script, and then just free-form answer the questions provided above while adding anything else that you feel is pertinent to establishing your why. Remember, you establish your why as a reminder to stay on the path no matter what it feels like.

Here or in your journal, write this on the top of a page:

I am here to pay attention to and eventually release:

Now start to write without editing or revising what you write . . .

_____

_____

_____

_____

_____

_____

_____

_____

_____

_____

After answering the questions in your journal, jot down some reasons to move forward, and what you want to leave behind.

Keeping it affirmative, compose your why statement here as it reflects what you have recorded. Write it clearly and definitively. Keep this statement to two to four powerful and clear statements or fewer.

Here is an example: *I choose to consciously challenge my conditioned self as it has demonstrated as shadows in order to be extraordinarily free, happy, healthy, and able to live in loving relationship to all.*

_____

_____

_____

_____

_____

My why:

_____

_____

_____

THIS BOOK EXISTS BECAUSE IT SERVES MY WHY, AND MY WHY IS ALL ABOUT EMPOWERING OTHERS TO LIVE A LIFE OF FREEDOM. YOU ARE PART OF MY WHY.

In order to embrace the stimulating influences of your why and stay focused on your desired outcome, you will need to cultivate *discipline*. The discipline that I am referring to is how to initially respond to the stimulus, the feeling, the re-action. Your first reaction will govern how this will flow for you. If your initial response is to blame someone, to resist the feeling and experience, or to distract yourself from what is happening, you will miss the opportunity to move through it with ease and grace. The philosophy of *Shadow Work: A Spiritual Path to Healing and Integration* requires that you consider letting go of the habit of blaming others in addition to any sense of righteousness, which is a real indicator of necessary shadow work.

Should you give in to the temptation of blame and accusations of another as the cause of your pain, you will extend the time of your suffering. These feelings are the stimulus that needs to be recognized and inventoried.

The difference between *feeling the stimulus* and *resisting the stimulus* is simple. When you are comfortable simply feeling what is stimulating your emotions, that speaks to your discipline and speaks to your ability to stay steady. This will encourage you to choose wisely. When you are resisting the stimulus, your attention is on the challenge and trying to avoid what it is you are feeling. You can't keep avoiding feelings and learn from them at the same time. If you are willing to feel the stimulus, you are positioning yourself to take stock in a conscious way of what is going on. If you resist the stimulus, distract yourself from it, or choose to dull the feeling of it through the intake of any kind of substance, you will be dulling the very feelings required to guide yourself to freedom.

IF YOU DON'T EMBRACE THE CURRENT OPPORTUNITY TO HEAL THIS SITUATION, HENCE THE STIMULUS, IT WILL REVISIT YOU AND OFTEN WITH A MORE INTENSE EXPERIENCE.

STORY TIME

Frank's Story

Meet Frank. Frank was happily married to his wife, Christine. They were a blended family, having one child together, a daughter, and two other children from Frank's first marriage. What Frank didn't see coming was Christine telling him that she wanted a divorce. He hadn't been paying attention, so he missed all of the clues that became obvious after the fact.

Christine chose to leave without any of the children, not even her own; again, all were shocked. This led to Frank caring for his three children as a single dad.

As time rolled on, Frank researched the best childcare situations for the two youngest ones, who were two and four, and after-school care for his older daughter. But soon Frank began to find reasons to complain about the care his children were receiving, and so he kept coming to one childcare facility after another, always finding fault. He was also dissatisfied with the after-school care for his older daughter. Basically, Frank walked around finding fault with every child facility in the same way that he constantly criticized his two ex-wives for the way in which they each parented.

A couple of years ago, Frank found his way into my Shadow and Forgiveness courses, and he was led to discover that his criticisms of the childcare facilities and his criticisms of his wives were a trauma response to being very neglected as a child. He grew up in a home with an absentee dad. Frank promised that he would never be that, but he didn't realize that his mother was a major culprit in his sense of self-worth.

As he worked to unpack all that had happened, Frank came to

realize that he didn't trust women in general, especially his mother, because of how poorly she had cared for him and his siblings. He was caught up in feeling unseen, and uncared for, which led him to feel unworthy of love. Frank chose to practice forgiveness: He forgave his father for leaving, his mother for being unskilled, and himself for allowing himself to suffer over all those years. He thanked the current people in his life for directing him back to himself and brought that shadow home.

Soon after, there was a fairly dramatic shift in his perspective. All of a sudden, he was seeing the childcare givers differently, appreciating their efforts and care. And he also took time to make amends with both his wives for being part of driving them away.

Practicing Radical Honesty

Practicing radical honesty is an invitation to simply say what is, to assess as objectively as possible what is happening on the landscape of your life without making excuses for it. Name it, claim it, heal it, and then get free from it.

Pay close attention to your body and its reactions; so much of the pain you experience is caught in the cells of your body.

The need for shadow work is very easy to recognize when we are dealing with others, when we see ourselves judging others, and when we are not tolerating the behavior of others.

A bit more difficult, but equally effective, is learning to recognize the need for shadow work as you access negative emotions that you express most often. Once again, realize that these emotions have been living within your subconscious as seeds causing certain behaviors.

Now, while practicing some radical honesty, use the empty chart on the next page of this book and fill out the pie chart. It is very helpful to have a visual in this process.

Remember that these emotions are not bad or wrong; however, it is likely that these and other such emotions do crowd out your ability to fill the fullness of your being.

The Wheel of Shadows

You will need a pen and a highlighter to use this chart.

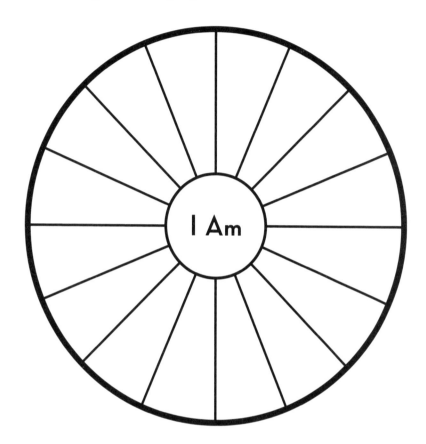

1. Imagine this wheel represents the whole you. Fill out the chart using the questions below. Make this a list of your enjoyable and challenging qualities. Mostly you want to focus on where you feel challenged. Place one characteristic or self-belief in each section of the pie chart above.

2. Using the highlighter, cover the tendencies and traits that create pain and discomfort within you. You will begin to see that the wheel is uneven. These highlighted parts are seeking to come home to you.

3. Use the script provided below for each and every piece of the pie that you covered with highlighter.

I am willing to look at, love on, and fully accept each feeling in my pie chart. I recognize each feeling as a puzzle piece leading me to wholeness. I accept (name the part) and call this part home.

Example: *I am willing to look at, love on, and fully accept each feeling in my pie chart. I recognize each feeling as a puzzle piece leading me to wholeness. I accept my jealousy and call this part home.*

To fill out the chart, ask yourself:

- Who are you, and what are you feeling about yourself?
- How do you label yourself, judge yourself, describe yourself?

Here are some things to consider looking at: the roles you play, the sins you have hidden, your emotional reactions, how you might play small, how you present yourself.

Remember—you are on a journey of self-investigation. Be curious like a child, willing to look at what is *without* judgment. If you need to, add additional sections to the pie chart.

Take the feelings/characteristics that most jump out from the pie chart and use those here.

Feelings I am most distracted by are:

(Describe in feeling words only. Stay out of your head.)

_____

_____

_____

_____

_____

_____

_____

_____

_____

_____

If each of these feelings were transformed, how would they demonstrate in your life? Take each feeling, and imagine the feeling as *not* running you but as having value. Now, how do you imagine them demonstrating themselves in your life?

_____

_____

_____

_____

_____

_____

_____

_____

_____

_____

Finding Value in the Shadow

What you might begin to realize at this point in the book is that all of your shadow aspects have value. Their value has everything to do with the root of the shadow and the polar opposite of the shadow and how it lives within you. Learning to look at your shadow this way will also help you to understand others.

Here are some samples of what you can find when you begin to look past the surface of the shadow.

Think of someone who is always controlling.	As someone who feels insecure, they try to control the outcome.
Think of someone who is always bragging about their accomplishments or acquisitions.	As someone who does not know their intrinsic value, they are seeking approval to fill a hole inside.
Think of someone who speaks critically about others who drink or do drugs.	As someone who is afraid of their past and was likely the victim of an alcoholic or drug addict, they try to distract from their own pain.

When you were young were you called bossy?	Only to become a leader.
Did you ever get accused of always having to be in charge?	Only to become an organizer of sorts.

Our shadow gets mislabeled because we have not learned to look past surface appearances or to engage someone compassionately. We must learn to look deeper and with love. So often we get caught in toxic thinking, judging, and condemning, all because we have an unconscious need to feel superior.

EXERCISE

Try looking at these examples of the shadow and imagine what the opposite side of the shadow would look like in someone's life. The practice is to look at what is happening while imagining yourself or another as fully healed from the shadow that is presenting itself.

LOOKING AT THE SHADOW	IMAGINING WHAT'S POSSIBLE
Example: If someone is unreasonably afraid of going out at night and acts out when asked.	Instead of thinking of this person as being difficult, we can assume that some kind of trauma left this person damaged with fear.
If someone is always grouchy.	
If someone hates to celebrate holidays.	

If someone always demands that they drive when going somewhere with a group.	
When someone always needs to be the center of attention.	

The more you practice, the easier it will be to see past the illusion of what we call the shadow. I call it an illusion because it is not who you are; your shadow is a reporting system. Humans don't come with user manuals, but we should, and if we did there would be a huge section on learning how to read your shadow.

Now let's make it more personal and take a closer look at some of your characteristics. On the left, name a characteristic you don't necessarily love about yourself.

The purpose is to see how the shadow/ your ego is trying to take care of you and stop condemning yourself. Practice seeing something objectively.

EXAMPLE: Sometimes I gossip and judge someone who is confident.	I look deeper and realize that I lack confidence and need to love myself as I am.

Now take a moment to appreciate yourself and the work thus far. You deserve to have this moment because the work you are doing is excellent.

You see, if you can become an expert at seeing the shadows—yours and other people's—for the lessons they bring instead of the havoc they cause, we will all begin to engage with each other in a more loving and compassionate way. Our acting out is the result of awkwardly trying to manage our life. This is another justification for practicing non-judgment. Practicing non-judgment prepares you to see past the illusion to what is more important—the healing.

CHANGE HOW YOU LABEL YOUR SHADOWS, AND YOU WILL BEGIN TO SEE A NEW YOU.

MINDSHIFT

Accepting Your Feelings as They Are

On this good and glorious day, I surrender into the intelligence of the One. I accept and allow this One to be the one and only power for transformation within my life. I am clear that this One avails Itself to me, through me, and as me always.

And I, fully conscious and aware, avail myself to It. I open my heart, my mind, and my beingness, allowing myself to align with this Presence as a guiding light and wisdom throughout my life.

As I continue my journey to return to wholeness, I begin to accept myself and all my emotions as they currently exist within me. I choose to lovingly look at and accept each feeling as an aspect of myself that is seeking to return home. I accept every feeling, no matter how hard or painful it has been within my past. Through this acceptance, I accept the path to wholeness as it is laid out before me, naturally, through this practice.

I declare on my behalf that all feelings are acceptable, have value, and are worth feeling. Through this experience of acceptance, these emotions no longer have to express themselves in such dramatic ways in other people.

I accept myself today in the most beautiful ways possible. I accept all my emotions and my feelings. I accept myself as I am and as I have been expressing myself throughout my life. I look at my past no longer as wrong but simply as the unfolding of my beingness.

I accept all of me and I anticipate the beauty and the value of what has been living within these feelings. I accept the empowerment that comes as a result of accepting what is.

For the full demonstration of the transformation of these feelings and emotions, I am so grateful. I surrender this word to the Law of Creation with great anticipation.

And I let it be so.

This is a suggested mindshift script to be used as a first response to a stimulating experience.

Use this script as you begin to feel something, but before you know what and how to handle the feeling.

You don't have to memorize it, but you will want to remember it as an example of what to do when the time is right. Your mind must be remolded, rewired, so to speak, to ready yourself for this whole new way of engaging your outer and inner life. Redesigning the way you see the work will help you overall. I want to help you change the narrative about shadow work and take away the mystery as much as possible. But, in order to do that, I need to give you the tools that will open the path.

MINDSHIFT

For Recognizing the Shadow

I know this experience is mine.

I don't have to like it, but I am willing to love myself through it.

So, I say to you, (name whoever has sparked this feeling): Thank you for inciting this feeling in me and for helping me to embrace a new opportunity to grow and find more freedom.

I see you and I recognize the opportunity to grow.

I feel into this moment and choose to be fearless in feeling it.

I bless you, (name person or feeling), for this invitation to grow.

I trust this path will lead me to my fullest expressed self.

I bless myself for having the courage to grow.

Follow the Feeling!

I am quite pleased with how today's psychology has learned to prioritize feelings—not as just some named emotion, but as a physical body sensation. This is key to understanding the full impact of your unhealed emotions, anxiety, worry, stress, and how they cause your health to be as it is.

Now that we have more focus on the true mind-body connection, we can be open to understanding ourselves in a better and deeper way. This deeper understanding positions you to heal faster.

Here is a beautiful benefit of this feeling method. Often, when one takes on this practice of looking for the earliest feeling memory, just seeing it helps one to release the pain and discomfort automatically. You see, when you look the feeling right in the eye, like looking under the bed for a monster, you are always led to find out that there was never a monster to begin with.

Facing our emotions is also like facing our fears: They will dissipate when you stand up to them.

All emotions have a specific and unique feeling texture. As you learn to identify your emotions by naming them, you will be led to the earliest feelings and memories required to create change.

The Process

When you are deep in shadow work and you need to identify a shadow, use this method to help.

1. Start with paying attention to the emotion that has been evoked from the work.

2. Sit in silence for a few minutes and call your entire attention to the feeling—not the thought about what is happening, just the feeling.

3. Now place all of your attention on the feeling, identifying where it lives in your body and the unique texture it has. While keeping your attention on

that feeling, let the feeling itself lead you to the earliest memory or at least feeling memory of that emotion. *TRY NOT TO THINK YOUR WAY THROUGH THIS.*

The beauty of this method happens when you allow the feeling tone to be your guide.

When you arrive at the earliest feeling memory you can get to, take note of a few things:

- How old are you?
- Where are you?
- Who is with you?
- What happened in that scene?

Once you have identified answers to all those questions, ask yourself these questions:

- What did I make this scene mean? (How we describe our memories creates meaning.)
- Is there anyone in this scene that needs to be forgiven?
- How did my ego help me avoid the pain of this memory?
- What parts of me do I get to retrieve as I call the parts back home that are incited by this feeling?

> **REMINDER:** The more expert you are about your inner landscape, the easier it will be to navigate your emotions and heal the blocks to your happiness.

The Road Map to Going Home

Start gently! Step one is all about setting yourself up for success. You will apply the noted spiritual practices and create a thorough inventory.

Up to this point in the book we have given you the why, the how, the what, and we have offered processes, tools, and skills that will be applied, but now the actual work starts. Everything before this moment was a warmup, the preparation. Now is the moment when your world and your intention to clear your shadow begin to become real.

This book and the program within the book are designed for you to have some freedom in deciding how fast or how slowly you move through. Definitely read all the material in the Getting Started section before heading to the processing. If you do the work, you will reap the benefits.

Although there is no promise that six weeks or six months of work will get you complete with all aspects of your shadow, fully applied (as guided) and practiced, it should leave you feeling hopeful and encouraged that you will have what you require to recognize, approach, and navigate your inner world, with the ultimate intention of bringing your lost and rejected parts home. Home is what we will refer to that inner landscape as.

It took a lifetime to create your shadow. Your shadow has been developing since birth and maybe before. This book has valuable information and guidance toward integration. But no true timeline can be served because you will notice aspects of your shadow as you are living your life. Some people go to therapy and shadow work becomes part of the conversation, but another way is to learn to recognize your shadow in everyday life and to embrace and engage it as it shows up.

The end result is the same, but if you approach shadow work proactively *while* staying fresh (the last part of this book is dedicated to maintenance), then you will be rewiring your brain and your emotional body to do this work in a loving and accepting way, even while you sleep. With the addition of the maintenance tools provided, you will be able to condition your subconscious to work on your behalf. There will come a time when the process will be so automated you won't have to do anything but notice.

Day 1. SKIP NO STEPS—every part of this journey matters.

- If you haven't done at least one week of pre-work, stop now and go back.
- Go to page 100 to set your intention.
- Go to page 101 to establish your why.
- Go to page 101 and sign the contract to be gentle with yourself.

And consider beginning each sit-down session with a mindshift affirmation or some silent meditation. This will make the journey focused but gentle. I have provided mindshifting affirmative scripts for your ease. Each step will contain prompts, principles, and practices for you to use throughout the week.

Take Inventory

Any journey that you decide to go on requires a couple of things. You have to know where you're starting from, and you have to know where you want to go. Without a clear sense of where you are and the trajectory of your desired outcome, the path can be unruly. We begin by using the tools of **contemplation**, **inquiry**, and **radical honesty**. Please make sure that you have a journal where you can write your deepest thoughts. Keep this journal safe. The safer you are, the more honest you will be with yourself. This is an important requirement for getting to your desired outcome. If you do not feel safe enough to expose your deepest thoughts and feelings on paper, you will avoid the work. Set yourself up for safety.

You will want to put aside quiet time to journal about the prompts below. Please take your time and stay aware of your body sensations. Remember, your body never lies, and it will help to guide what you need to know to move through your shadow work. REMEMBER—to the best of your ability, look at yourself honestly but without judgment. (You can already begin to see how important the practices are.) These practices come into play throughout your work.

Here is a list of some ways to recognize your shadow:

- Trends and patterns
- Health issues
- Unexplained anxiety (not related to an obvious stimulus)
- Triggers
- Body signals
- Reactions
- Unexplained movement toward or away from someone

After taking notice, name here the triggers and reactions that you experience more than others:

_____

_____

_____

_____

_____

_____

_____

_____

_____

_____

MINDSHIFT

Taking Inventory

To dive into the work without using these mindshifting affirmations is to do yourself a disservice. This shadow practice is different because we are engaging it within our spiritual essence and utilizing our relationship to the universe around us. These mindshifts take this work out of your head and move it into your heart, where it belongs. Love paves the path when we use the spoken word.

Use this *before* each session of taking inventory:

I sit and allow quiet, turning my attention away from the busyness of life and turning to my inner awareness. As I sit and get quiet, I open my mind and my heart to begin this journey of self-realization and self-empowerment. I take this journey one step at a time; I take it slowly and mindfully, while basking in the presence of perfection. Being grounded in the beauty of life itself, I ready myself for this journey as I affirm that I have the courage and tenacity required to walk gently yet steadily to my inner landscape, revealing all that needs to be revealed. I am ready to know myself more deeply, and so I practice radical honesty. I am ready to accept myself as I am and as I am not with sweet tenderness. I look without judging, and I feel all my feelings without shrinking back. I trust my process, and I allow this work to unfold with ease and grace.
Gratefully I release all fear.
And so I let it be.

Use this mindshift affirmative prayer *after* each session:

With gratitude, I appreciate the work I have completed as I celebrate my courage and my willingness to go deep while being gentle and kind with myself by withholding judgment. Yes, I am ready to move along this path of self-discovery. I affirm myself, I affirm my work, and I practice patience throughout this journey.

Those Dang Insecurities and Interruptions

Before you begin the actual process of taking inventory, let me draw your attention to something that could possibly get in the way. Humans indulge in all sorts of addictions and addictive behaviors in order to survive life, but there are two addictions that are very subtle and almost imperceptible. They are our addictions to being nice and to being liked.

As you read these descriptions, pay close attention to how they might become part of creating a shadow. This is the same process as when you disown a version of yourself and then project it onto another. These addictions exist because of a lifelong habit of self-disapproval. It is quite sad, but it is also rampant in our society. If all you got from this book was a desire to rise above these addictions, it would be a worthy read. You deserve to live an authentic life, which these addictions deny you.

Addicted to Being Nice

Let's look first at our addiction to being nice, because this one could easily get in the way of you practicing your radical honesty, and being radically honest is a cornerstone of this work. Most humans twist themselves into pretzels, denying their natural inclinations and needing to get approval from another. We spend so much time disapproving of ourselves that we seek to get approval from the outside. And this habit lends itself to creating your shadow.

I am encouraging you to pay attention to this addiction for a couple of reasons.

1. If this addiction is in full expression, you might not be honest enough in your private journal as you take inventory. And although I strongly encourage you to practice non-judgment, to be in this process, you must free yourself to see what your judgments actually are. If you deny them, you will be severing the connections required to feel what needs to be felt.

2. The other reason to pay attention to and to heal this addiction is because either you are being authentic, or you are not. If you are not authentic, you will stifle the shadow process. But this addiction is far reaching beyond shadow work. People who are inauthentic constantly agree to do things they don't want to do. They give dishonest opinions even when asked for an honest opinion.

Now, I am not telling you to be mean or unkind. Being nice in the world has its place, but not when you are trying to analyze and identify parts of you that you need to understand in order to find freedom from them. So please do be polite and nice to your children and your elders, but when you are looking inside yourself or if you are working in partnership with another for this shadow work, definitely pay attention to how often and how much you curb your opinions in order to get approval.

JOURNAL PROMPT: WHO DO YOU DUMB YOURSELF DOWN AROUND MOST OFTEN? WHOSE APPROVAL DO YOU WANT MORE THAN ANYONE ELSE? WHOSE NEEDS DO YOU PRIORITIZE OVER YOUR OWN? _____

_____

_____

_____

_____

_____

_____

_____

_____

_____

_____

_____

_____

_____

Being nice instead of being honest is paramount to denying yourself, yet there are times that raw honesty can feel hurtful. Be ready to have alternate ways of responding in those moments. Without alternatives in place, this new habit can be challenging. Here are some suggestions for alternate ways of responding:

- Hmm, let me think about that before I answer.
- I'm not sure I'm the best person to give you an opinion on this, but here's a thought.
- I have a few thoughts on this; would you be open to hearing a different perspective?
- Let's think about how this could work for everyone involved.
- I appreciate where you're coming from, but I might have some reservations.
- I think there might be different perspectives to consider here.
- I prefer you in a different color, but you must feel good about your choices.
- I really am not able to be honest here, because I am too close to you.
- I need time before answering.

All of these options or whatever else you come up with will give you a moment to pause.

Addicted to Being Liked

Closely related to your addiction to being nice is your addiction to being liked, but their elements are slightly different. Being nice is a bit more inward focused, but your addiction to being liked demonstrates itself in a social setting. Many individuals are socially awkward due to a lack of confidence, and so your desire to be liked will battle your insecurities. This causes you to agree to statements in a group just to belong (groupthink). You will find yourself not offering an authentic reaction when in conversation with others because you are afraid of saying the wrong thing.

Again, these habits/addictions create within you the temptation to hide and deny who you really are, and this is a great loss, because only you can be you. And when you begin to free yourself, you will begin to take note of how much of yourself you have been denying.

Practice some radical honesty:

- How often do you say yes to a favor when you really want to say no?
- How often have you had intimacy with another when you didn't want to?
- How often do you deny your true opinion to blend with a group or even one person?
- How often do you find yourself seething inside from unexpressed anger?
- How often do you let stress build up in you trying to satisfy an impossible task?
- How often do you deny your needs to please another?

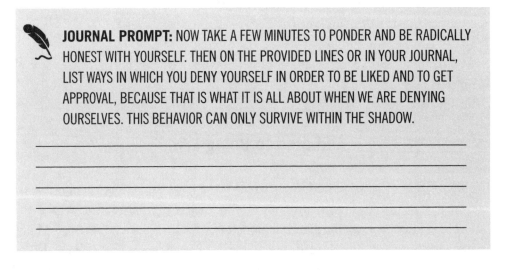

JOURNAL PROMPT: NOW TAKE A FEW MINUTES TO PONDER AND BE RADICALLY HONEST WITH YOURSELF. THEN ON THE PROVIDED LINES OR IN YOUR JOURNAL, LIST WAYS IN WHICH YOU DENY YOURSELF IN ORDER TO BE LIKED AND TO GET APPROVAL, BECAUSE THAT IS WHAT IT IS ALL ABOUT WHEN WE ARE DENYING OURSELVES. THIS BEHAVIOR CAN ONLY SURVIVE WITHIN THE SHADOW.

The more honest you are with yourself, the more powerful this exercise will be for you. Remember that anything that we deny, even our needs, if left unseen, will feed the shadow. All our unspoken expectations can also become part of our shadow, especially if we are blaming another. You are worthy of your authentic expression, and that is the goal here. You, being you, without excuses.

WHO DO YOU PRIORITIZE OVER YOURSELF AND YOUR NEEDS?

_____

_____

_____

_____

WHOSE OPINION DO YOU VALUE MORE THAN YOUR OWN?

_____

_____

_____

_____

WHAT PERSONALITY TYPE DO YOU TEND TO COWER TO?

_____

_____

_____

_____

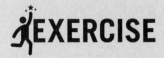

EXERCISE

Three Shadow Inventory Lists to Work From

Taking inventory is akin to reading a road map of your tendencies and challenges. It is important and can be challenging for some. As always, be gentle with yourself.

List #1: Seeing ourselves in others

Write down a list of people in your life that you most struggle with. This should be a list of current people and people with whom you have struggled but are no longer in your life. You still have strong feelings about them, their behavior, and how they show up in the world. (No one will see this list. Be honest. The more honest you are, the more complete the work will be.) Some of the people that you struggle with might no longer be alive, but the sheer mention of their name still evokes an emotional reaction.

One of the easiest ways to recognize this list is to pay attention to who you complain about, who you gossip about, who you are constantly judging when in conversation. (Now you can see why the pre-work was so important: You needed to be able to recognize your own behavior, hence your creations.)

Pay attention to:

- Anyone of whom you are jealous.
- Anyone you compare yourself to.
- Anyone of whom you are envious.
- Anyone whom you judge harshly.
- Anyone you feel nervous or anxious around.
- Anyone you gossip about.

These are great indicators to your shadow, and as I like to say, a gift waiting to be uncovered by you.

The more righteous you are, the greater the indicator that a shadow is lurking around the corner. Be incredibly careful, because righteousness can be quite blinding. If you find yourself being absolutely positively certain about someone as you call them all sorts of names, and can list their behaviors that are unconscionable, that is a surefire way to know that you have just found a shadow.

And I feel the necessity to say here that this is not the time to focus your attention on individuals, past or present, who have caused major catastrophic losses and events. We need to start with the smaller, more manageable shadows. Start small and build this skill over time. This needs to be all about you throughout this process. If you want to take on world events and leaders who have failed the planet, do that after you have made enough progress that your own shadow won't get in the way.

List the names of individuals with whom you feel incomplete.

_____

_____

_____

_____

_____

_____

_____

_____

_____

_____

_____

_____

List #2: Seeing your shadow in your emotions/feelings/reactions

This inventory is all about looking within, looking at your emotions, as compared to List #1 where we looked at the characters in our lives. As you look at yourself, look at your recent and not so recent reactions, and make a list of your most dramatically felt emotions. Pay attention to the things that get your attention, what causes you to react, what triggers can bring you from calm to almost insane, what trends and patterns of relationships you rotate through. What secrets about your behavior are you hiding? Reminding you again, if you feel tension in your body as you begin to recall things, pay close attention and do not deny those reactions.

If you are feeling unusually uncomfortable, you might feel tempted to stop, but don't—stay with it, feel all the feelings, and know that the feeling will pass. If you stop too soon, you will deny the feeling that will lead you to where you need to go in your inner landscape. As long as your feelings don't send you down a rabbit hole of self-criticism, stay with it. If you do begin to be overwhelmed, stop the inventory for a while and take on some of the spiritual practices that are listed at the beginning of the book, or simply start again tomorrow.

_____

_____

_____

_____

_____

_____

_____

_____

_____

_____

_____

List #3: Shadow and your regrets/sins/transgressions

This list is your regrets/sins/transgressions. Everyone makes mistakes, bad decisions, and has transgressions, some that might be current and many that are old. This is a time to forgive yourself but also to understand that our guilt and shame cause us to hide, and when we hide, we hide in the shadow. This is your most important list, and you could be tempted to beat yourself up—but DON'T, just don't do it. You are here to be free; looking at this list and feeling your feelings are part of your freeing process.

Regrets are caused from those decisions we make from some need to be filled, causing us to do something we would normally not have done. This is where we have to practice non-judgment again. Be gentle with yourself. Be compassionate. And remember, you would not have done these things if you thought you had a choice at the time. When we know better, we do better.

_____

_____

_____

_____

_____

_____

_____

_____

_____

_____

_____

_____

_____

_____

_____

_____

STORY TIME

Meet Amy, a Want-to-Be Actor

Amy, twenty years old, a feisty, confident, and talented young woman, decided that she wanted to go into acting. She had a lot of raw talent and entered a school of the arts. During her time there, her instructors were critical and unkind to her, saying things like "How do you ever expect to get work with thighs like that?"

This took place in the 1980s, and would be less likely to happen today, as we seek to have greater diversity in the arts.

Amy was devastated and left the school as she felt any possibility of pursuing her dreams was now squashed. Now she is a teacher, living a quiet life, and the closest she gets to performance is teaching performance in a local school.

Now, fully aware of all that has gone on, Amy has the choice of blessing the path that got her here and choosing not to take what happened in that very ignorant time personally. She can find peace now, but it is important that the path that got her here be acknowledged within.

Our shadows get created from a large variety of influences; in addition to everything I have suggested, also pay attention to your stifled dreams and unrealized goals. These, too, hide in our shadow.

Inventory Support

I have created a couple of forms to help you identify the personality types that you most react to. All these offerings are to help you shake the fruit of the tree so you can grow from them. After you do this inquiry work, go slowly taking the steps below. Try to eliminate any distractions for about thirty minutes as you focus.

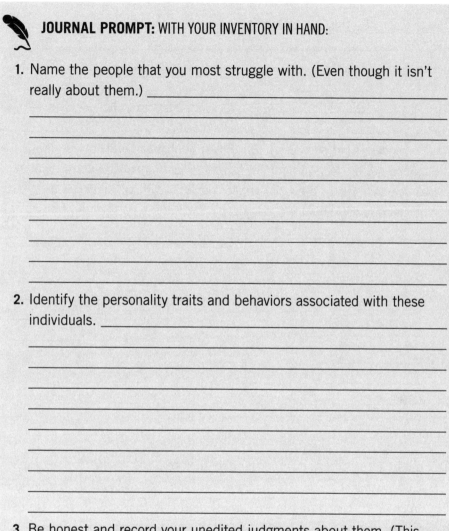

JOURNAL PROMPT: WITH YOUR INVENTORY IN HAND:

1. Name the people that you most struggle with. (Even though it isn't really about them.) _____

   _____

   _____

   _____

   _____

   _____

   _____

   _____

   _____

2. Identify the personality traits and behaviors associated with these individuals. _____

   _____

   _____

   _____

   _____

   _____

   _____

   _____

3. Be honest and record your unedited judgments about them. (This does not mean that your opinion is true or accurate, it is just your opinion; but again, you need to track your emotional reaction to them.)

   _____

   _____

   _____

   _____

_____

_____

_____

_____

_____

_____

4. What feelings get evoked as you think about these individuals? (Your feelings are the key component to understanding who you are. You will see patterns of these emotions throughout this inventory work. They lead to your shadows.) _____

_____

_____

_____

_____

_____

_____

_____

_____

_____

_____

Let me be clear here: You must understand that _the people that you listed in your inventory are not the problem, they are not the source of your pain and suffering, but they do provide a link to your shadow_ and when you follow it, you will arrive back to yourself. As I have said—there is no outside, there is no other.

Feelings, emotions, reactions, oh my. So much fodder to feel and to grow from. It can seem overwhelming, but the reality is that you have spent a lifetime avoiding feelings or not knowing what to do with them or how to handle them, so you stuffed them away, covered them up, justified them, or avoided them completely through drugs, alcohol, shopping, sex, food, etc. The combination of avoidance and stuffing is the culprit here. This is the first time that emotional health, emotional intelligence, honoring one's feelings, and recognizing the impact of stress as a trauma response have taken front stage.

Your feelings are a blessing to you, the lovely ones and the hard ones. It is time for you to learn to accept and not reject what you are feeling. Rejecting what you feel is how you got to this point in the first place. Most of us were reared in a household that had no understanding about the power of emotions, to say nothing about lacking the skill to allow you to process them. This doesn't make the people in your life wrong; they were simply unskilled. Most of us start out as unskilled.

Remember when we judge and condemn another, we are concretizing our opinions that in truth are hidden opinions about ourselves. As this process un-folds, begin to take on the practice of blessing the people in your life, every last one of them, especially if they have landed on your inventory, because they are your greatest gift. Yes, you could be righteous and continue to condemn them, but those condemnations only thicken the emotional block that you are here try-ing to move past. The question that you will always want to complete is this: As I heal this relationship, who do I become? What have I learned about my strengths by being in a relationship with this person?

Depending upon the timeline that you have set for yourself to do this work, you might be turning up the heat of emotions and could be activating emotions that might feel a bit overwhelming because of the intense focus. If you are will-ing to, slow down. Have a plan of action in place to practice some good self-care and tenderness. After a session of taking inventory, balance this work with doing something tender for yourself: Maybe go for a walk, or call a friend to chat. If you took my suggestion and invited a friend to do this work with you, this might be a suitable time to connect and share your work. Definitely remember to use the scripts for affirmative prayer mindshifts, because this is the magic of this particular shadow work.

Whether you are religious, spiritual, or an agnostic/atheist, using these scripts to guide your mind along a specific path is likened to Mary Poppins's advice, "A spoonful of sugar helps the medicine go down." Well, in *Shadow Work: A*

Spiritual Path to Healing and Integration, a loving and affirming spoken word softens the work enough to make it palatable.

Personal testimony:

> *I would not be who I am in the work that I do today if I did not healthfully survive my childhood sexual abuse. I do not wish this upon anyone. But since it is a part of my herstory, I might as well benefit from its presence in my life.*
>
> *This is what I mean by healthfully survive. While my early childhood is filled with an abundance of stories of violence in the home, explosive alcoholic moments, and secret sexual abuse, it is what it is. I cannot undo what happened to me, but I can control how I hold it inside, the way I relate to it, the way I report about it, and what stories I make up about it and how it reflects in my life.*
>
> *Our lives are not limited to what happened, not limited to our stories or memories. Our lives are the direct result of how we hold them in consciousness and how much power we give them. I will not be designed by my past, so I am always affirming my wholeness in this now moment. I do my emotional work. I practice forgiveness and recognize my shadow. And I know with great confidence that I arrived here not despite what happened to me but because of it. I bless the path that brought me here. I bless the people who were along that path, and I bless myself for my strength and courage.*

When your self-talk is kind and loving, you will always feel safe settling into who you are. You are the accumulation of your stories, your spoken word, and your invested emotions. But you must remember to stop judging yourself. Judging interrupts our healing.

How Do You See Yourself?

Here is another way to become more familiar with those pesky emotions that seem to surprise you or maybe those that you feel most often. The value of looking deeply into yourself is that you will become increasingly familiar with yourself and your emotions. This will benefit you in the long term as you learn to identify your emotions.

As Socrates said: "To know thyself is to have the keys to the universe." You have within you a vast wealth of information specific to you, to who you are, and the more you understand yourself and the causes of your life, the more self-compassion and self-love you can cultivate. Keep remembering this statement: *I am worthy of the work I am investing in and all the rewards that follow.*

🏃 EXERCISE

Practicing Honest Assessment

Answer these questions without thinking too hard—just let yourself answer them off the top of your head. You will need your journal for this.

When suddenly confronted with someone angry, I _____
_____.

When I am around a lot of people I don't know, I tend to _____
_____.

When I think someone has lied to me, I _____
_____.

When I am feeling unsafe, I _____
_____.

When I am alone in the dark, I feel _____
_____.

When I am worried about my children, I usually _____
_____.

If I face a challenge at work, my first response is to _____
_____.

When I feel overwhelmed by my responsibilities, I tend to _____
_____ .

In moments of uncertainty, I find myself _____
_____ .

If a friend or family member is in a crisis, I _____
_____ .

When I think about my financial future, I _____
_____ .

When I am confronted with a personal mistake, I _____
_____ .

If I feel rejected or left out, I _____
_____ .

When I experience a success or achievement, I _____
_____ .

If I am feeling lonely, I usually _____
_____ .

When I think about my health, I _____
_____ .

In situations where I need to stand up for myself, I _____
_____ .

If I am facing a difficult decision, I _____
_____ .

When I feel unappreciated or undervalued, I _____
_____ .

If I am anxious about an upcoming event, I _____
_____ .

When I reflect on my personal growth, I _____
_____ .

If I feel stressed about time and deadlines, I _____
_____ .

When I am enjoying a moment of peace and calm, I _____
_____.

If I am upset with a loved one, I _____
_____.

When I think about my past mistakes, I _____
_____.

Look over your answers, tune in to your body, and listen to that quiet voice filled with opinions inside your mind. How do you feel about what you wrote? And, very importantly, what do you make that mean about yourself?

STORY TIME

Meet Hannah, a Mother of Three from New England

Hannah took both my Forgiveness Course and the Shadow Course to work on a variety of family issues. One of the main sticking points for her was her brother-in-law. He was just a constant thorn in her side every time he was around. She couldn't put a finger on why but was upset with how consistently she and he would clash or do the opposite and avoid each other.

Through the courses, she focused her attention on him, identified what it was about him that was a shadow in her, forgave him for his behavior, and forgave herself for her role in this relationship. Soon after she completed the deep work, her brother-in-law was coming to the house for a visit, so she braced herself for their normal interactions, but lo and behold, when he walked in, he appeared to have changed. Yes, suddenly all of the uncomfortable energy and interactions between the two of them were gone. And this is still true a year later.

When you do this work and healing happens, it will look like the individual with whom you are in a relationship has changed, even though they haven't. You changed. You altered the alchemy between you. It will look miraculous, but it is not. It is what happens when you do the work.

Trauma as a Shadow

According to Gabor Maté, a physician born in Budapest, living in Canada, all humans have trauma—**all.** Maté teaches that trauma is not what happened to you, but it is the result of what happened inside you. Take a child who witnesses violence in her home. She does not have the skill yet to process the feelings that are invoked through what she is witnessing, so her feeling reactions get stored in her body. Her life goes on as normal, but of course she is dealing with a new normal that she might not even be aware of. Stored deep in her psyche, this memory shows up later in her life as a fear or disowned and rejected memory, possibly projected onto an unsuspecting partner. Until she is conscious of this shadow, she will likely attract people into her life to support her belief about relationships and violence, but she will believe that it is the outside world.

Our job is to follow the triggers that show up in our life—without judgment— and recognize that they are signs of the shadow in our own psyche, take ownership of it, heal it through cognitive recognition, and apply the practice of mindfulness and mindshift so our unwanted part can come home. Once home, it ceases needing to project itself onto another, and we can become whole once again.

Trauma and the shadow are intricately connected aspects of one's psychological and emotional landscape. Trauma refers to distressing and often life-altering events or experiences that overwhelm an individual's ability to cope and process.

The effects of trauma can cast a significant shadow over a person's life, as trauma often leads to the suppression of intense emotions, memories, and survival mechanisms that may have been necessary at the time. These suppressed elements can become a part of one's shadow, influencing their thoughts, emotions, and behaviors in ways that might not be immediately apparent.

For individuals who have experienced trauma, shadow work becomes a crucial pathway to healing. By acknowledging and confronting one's suppressed emotions, a person can gradually process and integrate these traumatic experiences into their conscious awareness. This integration allows for the healing and transformation of the shadow, reducing the emotional and psychological impact. It's important to note that trauma recovery and shadow work can be a challenging and sensitive process, often requiring the guidance and support of a qualified therapist or counselor. Please practice extreme self-care. I do not want to re-traumatize you.

Next Steps

When young, you might have had a big brother or an older cousin trick you by asking if you wanted to play 52-Card Pickup. If you don't know 52-Card Pickup, it is a very silly game where you entice an unsuspecting child to play and, once they say yes, you take a deck of cards and throw them in the air and then tell them they have to pick them up. Shadow work can feel a bit like that. I wouldn't be surprised right now if you're feeling a little bit like your head is in a spin, you have opened a can of worms, and you really don't like to do the work, and yet you know it is necessary in order to plot a course for wholeness.

Hopefully, you have followed my guidance and given yourself some rewards for simply creating the inventories and doing the work. Over my years in teaching this work to thousands of people, it is always quite surprising to me how unnerved they can get simply by creating the inventory. Sometimes they feel bad because they recognize that it's their judgment that has caused some of their discomfort, but they also come to realize that all change toward transformation exists within.

Waking up to who you have been while expanding your self-awareness can often come with an ouch. Yes, awareness is curative, but first it bites. And sometimes it bites hard. It is imperative that you do not activate shame by judging yourself. Please practice kindness. Waking up to who you are is the most loving thing you can do for yourself or others around you, but there is some pain and discomfort that comes with it.

This week or month, depending upon how quickly or slowly you have decided to take on this journey, we are now going to look a little deeper at the people on your inventory lists. What's going to happen is we are going to print the name of each individual on a separate sheet of paper in a journal and we're going to begin to apply the spiritual practices within this book to transform these individuals. Initially it might feel a bit complicated and difficult, but after your first few, you will begin to breeze through the process with great ease.

STORY TIME

Meet Grace and Steve—A Success Story

For teaching purposes, I will share with you a success story. Grace worked for her husband and his business partner, Steve. For some unknown reason, however, Grace and Steve did not get along at all. They were polite because they had to be, but she and her husband's partner did not see eye to eye.

When doing her shadow work, she discovered that one of her shadows was born out of the fact that as a young girl, her father cheated on her mother. Grace's father told her, and she had to live with that knowledge, leaving her feeling guilty as hell while betraying her mother. You see, Steve was a philanderer, and Grace had an awareness of this, because she worked in the office and would witness his behavior. She judged him strongly and felt guilty because she also knew his wife.

Now, for background on this, you need to know that not only did she have this unworkable relationship with Steve, but she also became an unfaithful wife. So, Grace was dealing with her shadow as projected out and then demonstrating the very same behavior that she was criticizing.

Years later, Grace found me and my shadow work and chose to dive headfirst into it. She was so brave that I was inspired. As she got to see that her guilt, judgment, and criticism about her father caused her to reject this personality type, and faced the fact that she too was indulging in this unfaithfulness, initially it was quite painful. But she practiced forgiveness for her father's influence, she forgave herself for the judgment and for projecting it onto another, and as she brought that guilt-ridden part of herself home, she found peace.

Not only did she find peace, but she also ceased judging that behavior, stopped participating in that behavior—along with forgiving herself for cheating—and she no longer needed to judge her husband's partner. She became free. Free does not equate with approving of the behavior, but it means she was no longer impacted by the philandering behavior of another. She was absolutely free.

Bring Your Disowned Parts Home

Here are a couple of scripts to support your process. Always consider recording them in your own voice and then listening to them at night right before you go to sleep. This can easily be accomplished with today's technology. If you have a phone, you likely have the ability to record.

MINDSHIFT

Bringing Our Parts Back Home

Fill in the blanks with the specifics for each shadow focus you have discovered.

Today, _____ (date), I, _____ (name), declare that the love and genius of this Universe empower me to create powerful change in my life. I consciously accept my Divine birthright. As I choose to face this shadow (name it here), I recognize who I can become as I invite this rejected part back home.

I bless this shadow as a source that has reminded me that this shadow exists. I release the pain and discomfort associated with it as I choose to feel it in a whole new way. I choose to consciously bring this once rejected part of me back home, home into my heart and my soul. No longer will I reject this part of me; instead I call it home, returning me to greater wholeness.

I bless all the feelings that it has ever sparked, and I forgive myself for giving the shadow any power to harm myself or another. I am worthy of this beautiful transformation. I am worthy of my wholeness and all of the ways I can now show up in the world as whole.

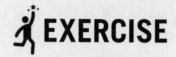

EXERCISE

Creating a Statement of Clear Acceptance of Your Good
Create a statement declaring the process as complete.

You're already familiar with crafting affirmations, and now, the world has begun to recognize the impact of thoughtfully crafted and regularly used positive statements. Just a few quick pointers before you dive in to tap into your unique source of strength, whatever that may be for you. Embrace your courage and creativity as you compose a powerful affirmation for yourself.

Designing an affirmation requires these elements:

- Use bold and brilliant language—language that excites you.
- Use language that is highly affirming in nature.
- Write it in the first person.
- Write it in the now—no future projecting.
- Use your imagination so you are shaken awake to who you are.
- Fill the statement with all of the passion you feel for your why.

Example: I accept every single ounce of my being as all parts of me are integrated into my beautiful whole self. I am whole and I am worthy.

Now, it's your turn: **BE BOLD.**

_____

_____

_____

_____

While I have provided some sense of direction for integration, it will take some time to feel comfortable with the process. Over time, and with enough practice, the process will begin to move rather quickly. One step will grow out of the other quite naturally. And there will come a time when you will be able to recognize what's happening and integrate all that is before you absolutely effortlessly. This is the goal. I do not personally enjoy any kind of self-help, human potential practices that are overly complicated. If you stay present to what you are feeling and not just think your way through, you will create in yourself a rewiring that simplifies the process.

What used to take months to process for me now can happen in a matter of minutes. I can now move from upset—identifying the shadow—to self-compassion and forgiveness that leaves me free in a matter of minutes. This is my personal reward for staying with it, for staying strong, for setting the bar of my intention so high that it drives my behavior, awareness, and choices. I get to bask now in freedom.

Now that you are about to move through your list one individual at a time, take a pause to prepare yourself.

Some reminders for you as you begin to take on the actual task of bringing your parts back home. Please trust this list. It is compiled from my years of experience. If it is on this list, it matters:

- Keep the suggested spiritual practices in place before, during, and after all of your past processes.
- Move slowly.
- Be gentle with yourself—NO judgment.
- Allow yourself to feel all the emotions that come without shrinking back; you will be okay.
- Stop when you need a break, and breathe throughout your work.
- Remember to enjoy the rewards you have set in place—they will help you to rewire.

❓ The Three Questions

These three questions pave the path from where you are now to where you hope to be, as long as you are radically honest and introspective with yourself.

The questions are:

- Am I that?
- Have I ever been that?
- Do I judge or object to that?

These **questions** asked by you about your reactions practiced with **radical honesty** will be the shortest path to embracing your shadow and bringing the parts back home. These questions also lead to you taking **responsibility** for your world. Let me explain.

QUESTION #1: AM I THAT?

When you see someone behaving in a way that you totally judge, find offensive, or react to, *before* you go down the road in verbalizing your disapproval, STOP and ask yourself: *Am I that?*

Radical honesty is required at this stage. Not to be radically honest is to cheat yourself of a perfect opportunity for healing. If the answer to this question is yes, I am that—well, you have just stepped into a gold mine of information about who you are, about your shadow; and with some additional effort, especially no self-judgment, you are in position to embrace a disowned part of you, which of course leads to wholeness.

What happens if your honest answer to this question is no? Then you go on to question #2.

QUESTION #2: HAVE I EVER BEEN THAT?

If you answered no to the first question, which means that you are not currently displaying the characteristics or behavior that you are noticing and not reacting to, if you remain honest with yourself, the question really is, *Have I ever been that?*

147

Have I ever acted this way or in a comparable way to what is now catching my attention?

If the answer is yes, then once again, you have now identified a disowned part of you that needs to be embraced and very likely forgiven. Remember, it is showing up on the outside because it was once rejected by you, but now you get to bring this part home, which leads to integration and wholeness. Wholeness attracts a completely different reality, although it will be a lifelong work in progress.

And what happens if your answer to that question is no? Then you go on to question #3.

QUESTION #3: DO I JUDGE OR OBJECT TO THAT?

This question is treated a bit differently from the others, because it can easily be overused, allowing the seeker not to take responsibility for the creation of the shadow. Let's break this down.

It is altogether possible that you have never displayed certain personality types that you struggle with currently, but if the theory is solid—and it is—that your outer world reflects your inner world and your disowned parts, then logically you are tied to this behavior in some way. Having strong opinions, judgments, and objections to a type of personality will cement you to that person or personality type. This is how this can happen.

Here is a personal testimony to demonstrate this point.

My mother was an alcoholic. It was not a pretty sight, but the other part about my mother being an alcoholic is that as I matured, my judgment was that she was weak and impotent. So while I have never had a drinking problem or substance abuse problem, I do have an aversion to alcoholics who are not in recovery. But even more, I have a disdain for feeling weak and impotent. This provides the greatest punch in my gut.

So applying the three questions in this instance looks like this: *Am I that?* No, I am not. *Have I ever been that?* No, I have not. *Do I judge or object to that?* Hell yes, I do! And I strongly dislike feeling weak or impotent in my life in any way. This feeling will cause me to reject anyone who displays these characteristics.

When we practice radical honesty and approach this process bravely, answering the questions honestly, then we will be led to our wholeness by forgiving and embracing the parts leading us back to ourselves, our wholeness.

These three questions live at the heart of this work. Practiced regularly, you will be able to see a shadow, ask yourself the questions, and be guided back to yourself quite quickly.

The deeper we look and the more honest we are, the more we must match the focus of the journey with self-love and gentleness. This following mindshift is written to support you as you continue to deepen your inner journey.

MINDSHIFT

Accepting All of Me

I call forth the love of all that surrounds me now to be my guide, my path, and my strength. I show up here for myself with total conviction that I am worthy, completely, wonderfully worthy. Worthy of my good and my transformation.

Never again will I ever, ever criticize or judge myself, not aloud and not to myself. Today is a day that I begin to look at myself in the mirror with great love, and with compassion. I honor my journey, and I credit myself for having the courage to look within as a response to my without. My awareness sees what needs to be seen, but I do remember not to give any power to it. My life reflects back to me all my lost and rejected parts, but every day in every way possible, I begin to love myself as I am, and I bring all of me home.

I walk, act, and respond differently, because my wholeness is at hand. I appreciate the law that takes my spoken word and acts upon it. With a bounty of unending gratitude, I release my word to be created as so.

And so it shall be.

Two Approaches to Shadow Work

Shadow work is an intricate, personal journey. To make this process as effective and resonant as possible, I offer two distinct paths. Both aim to alleviate your burdens, but the chosen route should mirror your personal needs and disposition. Your primary objective is to shift focus, release painful attachments, and elevate your inner light. The time you invest and the path you select are your decision.

1. Through Relationships

Understanding the reflection of your shadow in others can provide clarity. While it might seem counterintuitive to look externally when the work is internal, it's often easier to first see our shadows in our reactions to others. We look outside at others because it is simply the low-hanging fruit in this process, making it easier for your first time around this work.

Quick example: I have a problem with people who are petty, but if I am honest with myself, I find that I can be petty. So this begs the question of attention. Is it about another or about me? If I practice radical honesty and admit my pettiness, then I can choose to accept this about myself, alter my behavior, and stop judging myself, which will have me automatically stop judging others for their pettiness.

Key Steps:

- Identify Challenging Relationships: Recognize where you face friction or discomfort.
- Select a Significant Person: Prioritize someone crucial in your current life.
- Evaluate Your Judgments: Reflect on how you view or judge this individual.
- Self-inquiry: Ask yourself the three questions: Am I this? Have I ever been this? Do I strongly judge or object to this behavior? Your answers will determine what you do next.
- Emotional Analysis: Name the emotions this person evokes in you.
- Trace This Emotion: Think back to the earliest memory that has the same feeling texture.

- Integrate and Heal: Engage in forgiveness or utilize a mindshift to reintegrate this shadow part and show gratitude for its revelation.
- Consider Various Relationships: Be they marital, familial, professional, political, or intimate. Recognize that this process will have nuances as your experiences and wounds are unique.

2. Through Direct Emotional Exploration

Delving directly into your emotional shadows can be intense but incredibly rewarding. This method demands a certain level of emotional and spiritual depth. I would have to call this option advanced simply because you are not distracted by another and are focused completely on yourself, your emotions, your feelings. It takes a bit more focused attention; however, it is more direct and will leave you feeling more empowered. This is where our practice of taking responsibility comes in handy. All the practices I have offered play a part in the healing of your shadow.

Emotions to Explore

- Criticism
- Anger
- Jealousy
- Guilt
- Shame
- Fear
- Insecurity
- Overreactions
- Perfectionism
- Victimhood
- People Pleasing
- Control Issues
- Self-sabotage

While this list isn't exhaustive, it offers a solid foundation for an initial investigation.

Whether you opt to navigate your shadow through relationships or direct emotional introspection, both pathways are valid. The relationship approach often requires a longer commitment, as you're processing one relational dynamic at a time. In contrast, the direct method, though intricate, offers broader healing. Whichever path you embrace, the intent remains to reintegrate disowned parts of yourself and move toward inner harmony and peace.

Here is the difference between the two methods.

One method has you look at the people in your life with whom you struggle while the second method goes directly to the emotions. Using a combination of both methods is where most people settle. We do begin by noticing relationships because it is the broken aspects of our relationships that allow us to notice something wrong more quickly. To work with emotions alone requires that one be willing to take complete ownership for their experience. It's a powerful way to handle it, but it can take a bit more work to get there.

Integration through relationships

The hope for using this method is that, over time, you will look at people in your life that were once challenging but now see them as opportunities for happier living and easy relationships, because you begin to live with gratitude for what they bring to you. We work through our shadow this way knowing that individuals in our lives are angels, blessing us with an aspect of ourselves that has been waiting to come back home.

When noticing your shadow through relationships, you:

    a. Notice a challenging relationship.

    b. Name the person and the challenge.

    c. Name the feelings this person and challenge evokes.

    d. Ask yourself the three questions.

    e. Ask yourself this: Who do I become as I embrace this part of me?

f. Set your intention, use a mindshift affirmation and/or a ritual, and claim your good as your wholeness.

g. State your gratitude and claim your good.

Integration through emotions directly

Choosing to recognize your shadow in your emotions is incredibly empowering. Over time, with enough practice, you will never again have to be afraid of or choose to avoid your emotions, because you will be too busy valuing their presence in your life. Oh, to develop the mindset that your emotions are a gift—what a powerful shift. Combine this mindfulness with learning to read your body's messages, and you are ready to go.

a. Name the feeling and the challenge evoked.

b. Ask yourself the three questions.

c. Set your intention, use a mindshift affirmation and/or a ritual, claim your good as your wholeness, and ask yourself this: Who do I become as I embrace this part of me?

d. State your gratitude for what you have learned about yourself from this emotion and claim your good.

Recognizing Your Shadow

I have provided some tools to identify your shadow, all the while reminding you that even as you recognize your shadow in someone else, it is never about that person. As you look around at your world, just outside your world, and then even further out, you will begin to identify many personality types, some you like, but many that you do not.

Depending on how you label what surrounds you, your world can look very different. What about an individual who sees nothing but liars and cheaters everywhere they look? Can you take a quick guess as to what is hiding in that person's shadow? Remember, objecting to a liar does not make one a liar, but it is an indication that a liar impacted their life. Or another option is that they were a liar at some time in their life and have never forgiven themself for it.

Maybe this person needed to forgive a liar in her life, and as she does so the shadow will cease to exist. Remember, as we accept the parts back home, we cease needing them to show up as a shadow.

This is a critical step in your journey. This is the part where you begin to detach from your righteousness about what you see, and now your inquiry helps you to see who you are as whole, as including the shadow you are looking at. Every time you exchange blaming another for acknowledging their value in your life, you ready yourself for a transformative experience.

Over time, with enough practice and the rewiring of your thinking, your worldview will be altered. Your worldview acts like a filter that you see life through. The more self-loving, optimistic, and compassionate you are, the more you will see evidence of good throughout our world.

YOUR SHADOW EQUALS UNREALIZED ASPECTS OF YOURSELF—ALWAYS.

WE SEEK TO INTEGRATE, TO WELCOME OUR PARTS BACK HOME.

THE MORE INTEGRATION, THE GREATER YOUR PEACE OF MIND!

Below are examples of how we see the world differently once our understanding and worldview shifts. This is another reward of doing this kind of work. This will also bring you peace of mind. When you cease judging and learn to look past the behavior of others to see their motivation with compassion, then peace, ease, and grace are the rewards that you will reap.

Pre-understanding: At first sight, an angry, nasty person deserved your criticism.

With understanding: Now you know you are guided to love and accept yourself and others as they are.

Pre-understanding: Judging people for how they look.

With understanding: Realizing that you often judge yourself.

Pre-understanding: Thinking that all men are bullies, or all women are nags.

With understanding: You come to realize that you are dealing with old relationships that you struggled with.

Pre-understanding: Always feeling insecure around powerful women.

With understanding: Realizing in truth that you are envious, and now realizing it has nothing to do with them.

Remember that your ego projected this shadow onto others so you could plot a path home. Your ego loves you and wants to protect you, but how it gets created and how it displays itself can often be a mystery. The mind is a resourceful thing and, combined with your ego, it can create some interesting human experiences.

Your practices will strengthen you as long as you stay steady with them for a committed amount of time. Every shadow you conquer over your inner turmoil leaves you more powerful.

This is the time in your study where you will begin to understand how the parts—what appear to be the separate parts—work together for you on your behalf. You see your inner world projects and creates your outer world, but as you heal, the outer world reflects your healing. What a gift!

If beauty is in the eye of the beholder, then, too, your world reflects how you hold it and describe it.

- Do you look out and see your life as a happy place or as a challenge?
- Do you think of people as greedy and dishonest, or do you recognize the generous people of the planet?

- What you are seeing with is what you will see.
- How you judge yourself and your world is how it will be reflected. This is why it is *extremely important* that we not give power to anything outside of us.

The challenge with the shadow is the struggle to see and recognize it. The quicker you release your shame and self-judgment, the sooner you will be able to let go of your judgments enough to love and embrace it and welcome the part back home.

STAY WITH IT, PEACE IS ON THE WAY.

AFFIRM: As I grow in my understanding, I am more powerful in my healing.

Name That Shadow!

Naming your shadow can be a helpful tool in the process of self-discovery and personal growth. When we identify and give a name to the hidden or repressed aspects of our personality, we gain power over them, bringing them into the light of our conscious awareness. This process is crucial because what remains unacknowledged and unnamed often exerts an unconscious influence over our thoughts, emotions, and behaviors, affecting our relationships, decision-making, and overall well-being.

Naming your shadow is a way of demystifying and humanizing the aspects of yourself that you might have deemed unacceptable or uncomfortable. By putting words to these traits or emotions, you create a bridge of understanding between your conscious and unconscious mind. This awareness allows you to confront, explore, and ultimately integrate these shadow elements into your self-concept. As you name your shadow, you begin to take responsibility for its influence in your life, which empowers you to make conscious choices and decisions that are more aligned with your true self. In doing so, you pave the way for personal growth, self-acceptance, and a deeper, more authentic connection with others.

Moreover, naming your shadow facilitates the process of self-compassion. It helps you approach your hidden aspects with empathy and understanding, recognizing that these parts of you exist for a reason, often stemming from past experiences, fears, or unresolved conflicts. When you name your shadow, it becomes less daunting and intimidating, making it easier to work through these hidden elements and transform them into sources of strength and self-awareness.

Ultimately, the act of naming your shadow is a powerful act of self-love and self-acceptance, enabling you to become a more integrated and authentic version of yourself. This entire book and all the work is about you loving you more, because as I have said before, **hurt people hurt people, but healed people love, and love becomes your legacy.**

It is common practice in certain shadow circles to name your shadow parts. Because I am concerned that the unpracticed individual could get caught up in this process of naming the shadow and in some ways be distracted by the whole thing, it is not my common practice. So, I will offer you this version of naming that shadow that you might find helpful. Stay alert, though; the last thing we want to do is to create a sense of otherness.

While going through this process, there might be some shadows that are a tad more stubborn than others. For those lingering or troublesome shadows, identify the age you were when that shadow started. (You will find these by the feel and follow method I taught earlier.)

For example: You are currently struggling with a neighbor who you feel is unreasonable with his demands about the property lines, and all your communications are brusque and unkind. You find yourself being nervous with each interaction. After sitting down and naming the judgment that activated the feeling you experience with him, a memory comes to mind. How old were you at the time of the incident?

EXAMPLES: Take your name and the age to turn it into—
Rachel, my eight-year-old worried Nervous Nelly self. (Always attach your name to the characteristic so you can own it.)
Rachel, my five-year-old Scared self.
Rachel, my twelve-year-old Lonely self.

Naming the shadow and attaching your age to it will help you to identify it as it rears its head.

This part of shadow work can be a bit of fun. Once again, whatever it takes to create a shift in you is what matters. Take a look at your shadows that are trends and take a few minutes to list the name and age of the shadow.

SHADOW CHARACTERISTIC	MEMORY ATTACHED	AGE	NAME OF SHADOW
Example 1: Mean and unkind	Being bullied by kids in school.	11	Scaredy cat Michelle
Example 2: Criticizing smart people	Having uneducated parents and being ashamed of them.	10	Desperate Michelle

With all the steps we take, let's remember to keep it light. Keep your sense of humor intact. Completing these assignments should help you to identify your shadow so you can now partner with it. If you find yourself overwhelmed at any point, please seek professional support to do this work. Not everyone can do this work unsupervised; you must know your own limitations.

Two other names:

1. While naming the shadow might not be my preference, you might like the idea. So, if you do, create a name for your shadow, but one that feels loving and intimate. This might be created from looking at your inner child and naming that aspect of you.

2. Your Golden Shadow. If you are creating names, name your Golden Shadow also. That part of you that is ready to burst forth to be seen and expressed. He/she/they need(s) to be exalted as you do this work. (More on your Golden Shadow in the Maintenance section.)

Thank You, Shadow!

When you arrive at the place where you can appreciate the angel (your shadow) for showing you the gift of your shadow and how it has been interrupting your peace, you will know true peace. You are here to shift from blame, judgment, righteousness, and superiority to acceptance and appreciation.

Every person on your inventory holds in their hands a gift. This gift is them pointing the way to the part of us that has been rejected and denied only to be projected onto another and then fussed with. But once we understand that we are consistently dealing with our own minds, hearts, belief system, and human psyche, we look forward to the gifts. We will begin to appreciate the boss that intimidates us, not because we deserve to be intimidated but because we deserve to embrace whatever part of us is causing that shadow and celebrate our growth.

Yes, you grow in personal peace and power each and every time you heal from another projected shadow. With each shadow you reclaim, be calm, return to being grounded, and declare your personal power, more than you have in a long time—mostly because you have been hiding and judging yourself and your shadow.

Imagine this scene—and I do mean imagine, as a matter of being playful. Let your imagination see each individual in this scene as a cartoon characterization of themselves.

See yourself walking into a party on a summer day—maybe it's your friend's child's birthday. And every time when meeting a new person (they all look like cartoons), when they reach out to shake your hand, instead of the old "How are you? Nice to meet you," they say, "Hi, I'm here to annoy you and offer you the gift of patience."

Or try another:

- Hi, nice to meet you, I'm here to help you see your stubborn side.
- Hi, I'm here to show you just how much you hate arrogant people.
- Hi, I'm here to remind you of how much you have grown and how you can handle alcoholics.
- Hi, I am so happy to be a glowing example of who you know you can be. (This is for our Golden Shadow.)

IMAGINE THAT EVERYONE YOU MEET ALONG YOUR PATH IS THERE TO GIFT YOU A DISOWNED PART OF YOURSELF, AND YOU ARE IN THE LIFE OF OTHERS TO HELP THEM CLAIM THEIR DISOWNED PARTS. THIS IS THE MAGIC OF THIS WORK, AS LONG AS WE CAN RESIST BLAMING ANOTHER.

Both love and gratitude are very healing personal qualities. When we use them together, for such a sacred practice, the alchemy of our life begins to change for the better. Let me demonstrate this idea. (Again, names have been changed and permission received to tell this story.)

STORY TIME

Meet the Fussy Neighbor

One of my students, Sheila, came to me with a struggle around a shadow she had identified. After some conversation with Sheila, it came out that she was intimidated by her own power that shows itself as this shadow. She was uncomfortable because after a small disagreement with her fussy neighbor, she did not like the way she was feeling about herself or the situation.

Once we identified the feelings that were activated by this neighbor and this event, we tracked her experience back to her youth, and could see very quickly that she had been dealing with some internalized trauma that this neighbor triggered—although innocently.

As soon as we identified her shadow aspects and the emotions that she was dealing with, Sheila was able to turn her attention away from her neighbor. She looked inside, tracked the story to an early memory, and could now see her survival mechanism and why it was created. She could also see that she would be far more empowered to deal with this fussy neighbor if she embraced her shadow to feel stronger.

So, now, instead of trying to figure out why her neighbor was making life a bit challenging in the neighborhood, she turned her attention inward as I began to offer her this language. This is spoken in the first person for Sheila.

Right here and now, I begin by thanking my neighbor. Yes, I appreciate him for being the angel in my life he has now shown himself to be. I am grateful for seeing a part of me that I have judged and rejected. As I move forward with mindful intention, I see and accept this part of me back home. I begin to see more and more what is possible when I choose love and acceptance over judgment and righteousness. Thank you, neighbor. I now stand here more whole and ready to move forward. I can even trust that our next engagement will be loving.

MINDSHIFT

For Integration
Use this mindshift as an example and write one in your own words below:

Thank you, _____, thank you for being in my life and showing me this part of myself that I have rejected. I can see now that embracing this part and bringing it home will guide me toward my wholeness. I am sorry for blaming you for my discomfort and not taking ownership of this experience. I do so now, and I do so proudly and eagerly as I walk home toward my wholeness.

_____
_____
_____
_____
_____
_____
_____
_____
_____

And practice here being grateful. Fill in the blank spaces. (Remember the cartoon faces.)

Example:

Thank you, <u>Mary</u>, for showing me <u>that I can be a bully sometimes</u>.

Thank you, _____, for showing me _____
_____ .

Thank you, _____, for showing me _____
_____ .

Thank you, _____, for showing me _____
_____ .

Thank you, _____, for showing me _____
_____ .

Thank you, _____, for showing me _____
_____ .

Thank you, _____, for showing me _____
_____ .

When you take time to reframe how you think and feel about someone, you will find some more freedom naturally flowing your way, because you are learning how to get on the other side of your challenging relationships and will create a new reality for yourself.

AFFIRM: I am grateful for all the people in my life who have grown me.

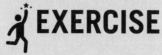

EXERCISE

Letter Writing

Write a letter to your entire shadow, thanking it for its help in who you are becoming. Name the shadow for this practice so it becomes intimate and familiar. Make sure that you are sincere, which means once again, check in on your body. Write until you feel a shift due to your shift in consciousness. _____

_____

_____

_____

_____

_____

_____

_____

_____

TO BLESS AN INDIVIDUAL, SITUATION, OR EXPERIENCE IS TO RECLAIM THE SPIRITUAL POWER THAT YOU POSSESS AND RECREATE A MORE LOVING EXPERIENCE!

To Bless Is to Reframe the Shadow!

For the simpler aspects of your shadow, choosing to bless all the components might not seem too challenging. After reading this section of the book, take time to practice, and make sure you begin with something simple (not a tissue issue). If this whole shadow thing is a new concept for you, you definitely need to start easy. You will want to move slowly through this practice. It is powerful, but it does require some practice.

Here is what the art of blessing does to any given situation. To bless, one must assume that they are a vessel through which all the uplifting and loving vibrations that exist are available to move through. To bless, first, one must be a receptor of this good so they can focus it on a desired outcome. So, to bless is to receive first and in advance.

Blessing another has the power to alchemically alter the vibration from dismal to hope and possibility.

If you choose to bless the food that you eat, you are spiritualizing it, and it becomes something healthy for you. If you bless your children when they begin to drive, they will be surrounded by love and protection. If someone is ill and you bless them, you trust that their natural healing abilities will carry them through. All of these acts of blessing are common and easy to understand. Where it might get tough is when I suggest that you bless the perpetrators in your life. This is where the rubber meets the road.

To bless something is to reframe how you name it, claim it, and experience it. Just as beauty is in the eye of the beholder, so is all of life. How you see something, which means the opinions, judgments, and experience that you bring to the table, impacts what you do see. If you are a believer that all people are good at heart and are worthy of love, then you will engage all that way. You will see their essence first and want to speak to that part of them.

But what happens when I encourage you to bless your perpetrators, the people who are instrumental in the creation of your shadows? Or how do you feel about blessing yourself and your transgressions? Can you find compassion for yourself to feel worthy of your own blessing and forgiveness? Just as one of the cardinal rules of *Shadow Work: A Spiritual Path to Healing and Integration* is there is no outside, there is no other, another is to be kind to yourself throughout the process.

As you glean the courage to bless someone who has been part of your challenges, you convert them from being against you to being for you. (Remember it has nothing to do with them, it is about how you hold them inside.) When I contemplate my father and bless his role in my life, I soften the space between us, and then he can have safe passage through my mind and heart. And each time I convert a feeling by offering a blessing, I am creating an alchemical change in the relationship, and you can do this, too. When we bless, we are not doing it from an intellectual place but from a whole-body marriage of truth and love.

Each time you choose to bless something in your life that challenges you, you are reframing the situation, and if you are open and receptive, you will find the wisdom within you to see these challenges as stepping stones to your wholeness and freedom, and not as something blocking your way. To bless is to reframe, and to reframe is to consciously choose what you see as you ponder life. When you are in this state of mind and ask one of the many questions that open the flow within you, even those who appeared to harm you will now be a gift (albeit disguised) for you to learn something new and amazing about yourself.

And once again, using practices like meditation, mirror work, and inner child awareness work will bring the unknown and the unacknowledged forward to be worked with. Developing a center of calm will always benefit you, because when your emotional waters are calm, you can see deeper into yourself, which is necessary as we are trying to identify our higher truth.

Here are some examples of this practice:

BEFORE: I hate my father for how strict he was.
AFTER: I ~~hate~~ BLESS my father for now I know how strong I can be.

BEFORE: I am so angry with my sister for stealing my boyfriend.
AFTER: I ~~am so angry~~ BLESS my sister for showing me how desperate I am not, and now I know that the right love will always be mine.

BEFORE: I can't stand my mother and all of her manipulations; I'm angry all the time at her.
AFTER: I ~~can't stand~~ BLESS my mother because I have learned how strong and resilient I am.

BEFORE: My family never saw, empowered, or encouraged me. I don't care if I ever see them again.
AFTER: I BLESS my family, because now I have learned to be strong, independent, and to take nothing personally. I am free.

BEFORE: I hate my boss for being such a liar.
AFTER: I ~~hate~~ BLESS my boss, because I now know he is not capable of being any different, and I free myself to attract a new position where I am appreciated.

BEFORE: I will never let someone in that close again.
AFTER: I BLESS all around me who taught me how strong I am.

BEFORE: I hate my mother for being an alcoholic.
AFTER: I ~~hate~~ BLESS my mother, because I know she was in pain doing the best she could.

SHIFT THE ENERGY FROM BLAME AND CONDEMNATION TO BLESSING, AND THE GIFT PRESENTS ITSELF TO YOU.

Now It's Your Turn

Take the first five names on your inventory list #1 and, using the suggested form below, apply this practice. While this practice is coming initially from your head, do it mindfully and slow down, and pay attention to the impact on your body—remember the body never lies.

Take the top five names, and fill those names into this form.

1. I bless (person's name here), as I take back my power. In blessing him/her/them, I soften their impact in my life.
2. I bless (person's name here), as I take back my power. In blessing him/her/them, I soften their impact in my life.
3. I bless (person's name here), as I take back my power. In blessing him/her/them, I soften their impact in my life.
4. I bless (person's name here), as I take back my power. In blessing him/her/them, I soften their impact in my life.
5. I bless (person's name here), as I take back my power. In blessing him/her/them, I soften their impact in my life.

Read your statements slowly, feel into them, and benefit from this mindful practice. You cannot be focused on being blessed and feeling the pain of the situation simultaneously. Allowing yourself to bless this person shifts your perspective, and you benefit from it differently. A sincere blessing is a beautiful gift that you give to yourself and the individual that you are blessing.

Gratitude and Your Shadow

Because the word *blessing* (like the word *God*) can be a trigger for many individuals, the essence of blessing is gratitude. I want to show you how to use these practices to soften your hold on your shadow and open the path to wholeness.

Choose to be grateful for the individuals in your life and how you have come to know yourself because of them. This way you will create habits of appreciation, healing, and optimism from the most unlikely situations.

At this point in the book, your view of how your world was created and is working now has been altered; your mind has been opened. You are beginning to see that the people in your life who pose challenges are a benefit to you. You have begun to process your emotions differently and hopefully more easily. You have less intensity about the people in your life whom you originally saw as the problem, the culprits. You can see that they live inside of you.

AFFIRM: I am grateful for this shadow and all that I have learned about myself because of it.

To Shift Your Focus

Start by shifting your focus from the darkness of your shadow to the positive aspects of your life. Each day, make it a habit to identify and write down things you're grateful for. This can be as simple as appreciating a supportive friend, a beautiful sunset, or a personal accomplishment. The act of counting your blessings begins to change your perspective, helping you see the brighter side of life even amid shadow work. Just as beauty is in the eye of the beholder, your reality is in the mind of the observer.

AFFIRM: My entire shadow is a beautiful aspect of me, and I choose to love it.

Reflect on Growth

Practice gratitude by reflecting on how your shadow has contributed to your personal growth. The hidden aspects of your personality stem from past experiences, traumas, or unresolved emotions. Acknowledge that these challenging experiences, while difficult, have shaped you into who you are today. Express gratitude for the resilience, strength, and wisdom you've gained from confronting your shadow. This perspective helps you view your shadow not as a burden but as a valuable teacher.

JOURNAL PROMPT: I RECOGNIZE MY GROWTH AS IT SHOWS UP IN MY LIFE AS . . .

_____

_____

_____

_____

_____

_____

AFFIRM: I have the strength and resilience to keep on going!

Cultivate Self-Compassion

Gratitude that is directed inward fosters self-compassion during the process of shadow work. Instead of self-criticism, embrace a grateful attitude toward yourself. Recognize that your shadow aspects, though difficult, are a part of your human experience. By appreciating your effort and willingness to explore and heal these hidden facets, you nurture self-love and acceptance, which are essential for integrating the shadow into your self-concept.

🏃 **EXERCISE**

Write about what aspects of yourself you are now willing to have compassion for:

_____

_____

_____

_____

_____

YOU ARE WHO YOU ARE NOT DESPITE YOUR EXPERIENCES BUT BECAUSE OF THEM.

AFFIRM: I am profoundly worthy of my self-compassion!

Forgiveness and Your Shadow

This section will teach you how to take responsibility for the creation of the shadow and use forgiveness for a transformative formula.

In my first book on forgiveness, *Forgiveness: A Path, a Promise, a Way of Life*, you will find a much more exhaustive look at forgiveness and how it lends itself to the personal journey of finding freedom as a support to shadow work.

If you really want to be free, forgiveness is a critical spiritual practice. Forgiveness is one of the most important tools for shadow work, because it is forgiveness that will help you to break the chains of connections between the persons or events that happened in your life and the creation of some of your shadows. Your job here is to forgive yourself for giving your power away, or for your judging, blaming, and fault-finding that has been part of this process.

Let's return to the Grace and Steve story. For Grace to heal from this internal emotional imprint to find freedom, a few things were required.

1. She needed to take ownership of her shadow by first realizing that it was a rejected and projected part that was alive in her because she judged her father (understandable, of course). This caused the guilt she felt from holding it as a secret from her mother.

2. She needed to forgive her father for having this affair in the first place, and she needed to forgive herself for keeping it a secret. Only through a deep forgiveness process was she able to cut the chain of pain. Once forgiveness was applied, the space within her was opened up for a shift.

The shadow shows up in the places where we need to practice forgiveness; they go hand in hand. Without a practice of forgiveness, you might continue to blame yourself. Remember when we blame, we suffer; but when we take responsibility, we are empowered to create change. The deeper you go into this work, the gentler you must be. A sign of being gentle will be your willingness to forgive yourself, especially when you are convinced that you do not deserve forgiveness.

I can share with you that some of the regrets in my life that have caused me to feel shame were not things that I thought I should be forgiven for. I was convinced for a very long time that I did not deserve to be free from my guilt and shame. Forgiveness felt like a luxury that I did not deserve. (Notice here that while you might be feeling something, it does not make that feeling your reality.)

Can you relate to this feeling? Are there things that you have done in your life that you are now realizing caused your shadow, things that you do not feel worthy of being forgiven for? This can be an extremely debilitating feeling, one that leaves you frozen. Keep going here. Even if you think that, it doesn't make it so, it is only your opinion about yourself, and that opinion will change as you move through the work.

STAY FOCUSED ON THE FACT THAT YOU DESERVE TO BE FREE.

It is important that we mention a few things here about forgiveness.

- Forgiveness is never, ever about the other person.
- Forgiveness is for you, for your freedom.
- Forgiveness is never about condoning behavior or about making excuses.
- Forgiveness is for your peace. Peace in your mind. Peace in your heart.

Forgiveness is like blessing someone in that it works at deep levels in our emotional body, and you might not be able to make sense of how it works. What I do know is this: When we begin to forgive, our heart is more open, our minds begin to relax, and the relationship that we are struggling with begins to transform.

Who are we forgiving and why?

1. We forgive the people in our lives who have left an imprint. These people might be innocent of negative intent, but that does not prevent their actions from having an impact. We forgive to be free, not to free another or to forget about their actions. We are simply letting go of making them wrong, so we have the energy to find our right. All individuals will have to experience their own karmic debt.

2. We forgive ourselves for our errors, mistakes, transgressions, for giving our power away, and for suffering long beyond the reasonable time that one should suffer as a response to a given situation. As we do this, we lessen our hold on our righteousness, and our attachment to being superior.

The vibration of love, forgiveness, and acceptance has almost magical effects. Today we can enjoy the fact that science supports the impact of forgiveness on the body. And as you practice and learn to appreciate this vibration, it will become its own reward, because you will begin to live a lighter, happier life all around.

> "Forgive yourself for not knowing what you didn't know before you learned it."
>
> —Maya Angelou

Here is an exercise and some language to quiet the emotional waters that are associated with your shadows. Set aside undisturbed thirty-minute time slots for you to do this work.

We return once again to our shadow inventory #1.

1. Take your list in hand and choose a name/shadow to begin with.
2. Sit quietly for five to ten minutes as you set the intention to be present, to feel, and to listen.
3. Name the most prevalent feeling that you are feeling as you contemplate this shadow/person. We never want to be ignorant; naming the feeling keeps you plugged in to yourself and the whole process.
4. Ask yourself this: Who do I get to become as I bring this shadow home? You must answer this question, as it will become part of your new conscious way of being.
5. Use this script to start your forgiveness practice with each name on your inventory.

> *I consciously choose to forgive _____, and I do so for myself and my peace of mind. I forgive them and trust they will clean up their own mental/ emotional debt, but I am free because I choose to be. I choose to let go. I choose to forgive this individual so I can be made free.*
>
> *I am no longer at the mercy of this memory, these feelings, of this individual.*

While I am able to name and feel my feelings, I am not at the mercy of them. My life now reflects my choice to forgive and let go. I forgive all the influences and call my shadow back home. I now walk taller and more confidently knowing I am free.

Fully healed, I now enjoy myself as fully realized and fully expressed.

Again—over time, this process happens very swiftly as long as you do not blame another outside of you.

MINDSHIFT

Suggested Steps for Processing Forgiveness
Step one: After looking over my list, I choose a shadow of a liar and a cheat. Someone I will call John for this purpose.

Steps two and three: In quiet meditation/contemplation, I get in touch with everything I feel about this person and this shadow. I choose to release John from all my judgment of him as a cheat and a liar, recognizing my own tendencies and taking ownership for also behaving in this way.

Step four: As I forgive John's influence in my life, I recognize that, fully integrated, I become a woman of high integrity and model this behavior in all that I do. I feel relieved.

Step five: Repeat this mindshift.
I consciously chose to forgive John, and I do so for myself and my peace of mind. I forgive him and trust he will clean up his own mental/

emotional debt, but I am free because I choose to be. I choose to let go. I choose to forgive this individual so I can be made free.

I am no longer at the mercy of this memory, these feelings, or this individual. While I am able to identify and feel my feelings, I am not at the mercy of them. My life now reflects my choice to forgive and let go. I forgive all the influences and call my shadow back home. I now walk taller and more confidently knowing I am free.

Fully healed, and integrated, I now enjoy myself as fully realized and fully expressed, and I celebrate this moment of transformation in me.

Continue to set time aside and process slowly and gently. For the shadows that carry a bigger impact, you might want to schedule a bit more time to feel into the process and plan an immediate albeit simple reward. Remember, reward to rewire.

Self-Forgiveness as a Magical Tool of Healing

You have spent your entire adult life trying to function on top of dysfunction. You have normalized a certain amount of pain and discomfort. You have never stopped to question if this current state of suffering has to be your experience at all—until now. This is not the only way to find yourself fully realized. Shadow work and forgiveness work are just two options, but these two options run deep and can cause a major shift in your consciousness. As your consciousness shifts along with your attention on your desired outcome, your life will follow suit.

Forgiveness complements shadow work because it removes the thought seed that influences your subconscious and your pain-body.

Forgiving yourself will help you to let go of the judgments stored inside and free you to recreate yourself by design and not by default. You can do this by using a mirror. The impact will be increased as you look yourself in the eye. If any of this language does not complement your language, then please just alter the statements. These statements are the result of years of working with individuals, but it must be your language, something that moves you; you must feel it, or it will have no influence.

While looking in the mirror, say:

- I forgive myself for not noticing my own suffering for all these years.
- I forgive myself for being judgmental and in so doing, causing the creation of my shadow.
- I forgive myself for not taking responsibility for my creations and then for blaming another.
- I forgive myself for not knowing what I didn't know until now.
- I forgive myself for blaming others who kept my power outside of me.
- I forgive myself for my part of the creation of my life, and I choose to accept myself exactly as I am and as I am not.

Create your own affirmations of self-forgiveness, while offering specifics:

_____

_____

_____

_____

_____

Shadow Inquiry Steps

Part 1: Setting the Stage

1. Name of your focus: <u>(name of the person sparking this feeling)</u>

_____

2. Describe the personality traits regarding this individual and all your judgments about them. (This is not the time to be nice; you must release all pent-up emotions.) _____

_____

_____

_____

_____

_____

3. Now, list the emotions you are experiencing as you think about this individual. (Feel your body. You want to list your emotions, not your thoughts.) _____

_____

_____

_____

_____

Part 2: Applying the Three Questions

Ask the three questions as you continue to pay attention to your body, because as we have learned, the body never lies.

The three questions:

- Am I that?
- Have I ever been that?
- Do I judge or object to that?

4. Take a few minutes to sit and follow the feelings that have been evoked. To be clear, the purpose of this step is to follow the specific feeling that has been evoked down to the earliest memories you have that feel the same. Try to leave this part of the process with identifying approximately how old you were at the time of the memory. (All emotions have a unique emotional texture; this is what you are identifying and following.)

You might need to take a few moments to breathe and get grounded after this part of the work. Pay attention to what you are paying attention to and to what your body is telling you. _____

_____

_____

_____

_____

_____

5. After you have identified the shadow, the feelings, and the memories, now begin to shift your mindset about this individual by pondering the answers to these questions:

- As I bring this part of me home, what becomes possible for me?
- How can I show up as I heal this emotion?
- What gifts has this shadow afforded me?
- Where do I need to forgive to be free of this discomfort?
- As I release blame and practice forgiveness for this individual or feeling, what aspects of myself can I now express and celebrate?

_____

_____

_____

_____

6. The shadow is created out of rejecting an aspect of ourselves and projecting onto another. Now you are imagining what, if that part of you were to come home, is ultimately possible. This is all about homecoming. Use your imagination.

JOURNAL PROMPT: AS I EMBRACE EACH OF MY PARTS BACK HOME, SOMETHING WONDERFUL BECOMES POSSIBLE FOR ME. IT IS . . .

_____

_____

_____

_____

Bringing the part home example:

I accept this part of me home, recognizing that I am worthy of wholeness; as I integrate, I am empowered.

Here is an example of applying the process.

Barbara Jones

Barbara is cocky and arrogant and walks around like she owns the place. I admit that I judge and object to that kind of behavior.

I feel insecure, and all of my feelings of not-enough get sparked when I am around her. I am envious of what she has accomplished. (I asked the three questions and found out that sometimes I strongly object to her behavior while wishing that her success were mine.)

As I take time to follow these feelings, I am led to an early time in myself when I walked around embarrassed about my mother, my father, and my family in general. We were a lower-income family, without any higher education. My family was not an inspiration to me in any way. And I have no memories of ever talking about anything that would help me to feel confident in my life. Jealousy and envy were rampant in my home, and I can remember being about five years old when I felt like it wasn't safe to be bold or independent.

I can see that this shadow has everything to do with me feeling less when I was young, less than anyone, especially Barbara, and feeling that way all the time. Now, aware of my shadow and calling this part of me back home, I look at Barbara, and I am reminded that it is okay to succeed, to be confident, and to walk around in the world believing in myself.

Right now, I choose to thank Barbara for shining light on this part for me, for reminding me that I, too, am worthy of believing in myself as I engage the world. I bless her for bringing me back to myself, for reminding me of my value. And I consciously forgive my mother, father, and family for not having the skill to uplift me, and I forgive myself for suffering and for not seeing my value sooner.

DECLARATION: I thank Barbara and accept the redirection of my attention as I claim my disowned parts of me back home. I celebrate feeling confident and worthy of success.

PRACTICE PAGES

Going Directly to Our Emotions: Option 1

Blank Process Page

Take the first name on your inventory and work through these steps. The explanations for each step are on the previous pages. Reminder: Be gentle, compassionate, and loving. I have provided six empty pages for you to practice on.

SHADOW WORK

1. Name the focus: _____

_____

_____

_____

2. Describe my judgments/reactions: _____

_____

_____

_____

3. This is what I am feeling and what my body is feeling: _____

_____

_____

_____

Now, ask yourself the three questions honestly. (Am I that? Have I ever been that? Do I judge or object to that?) My answer is: _____

_____

_____

_____

4. Bouncing off of the honest answer you gave, ponder this: As I recall this feeling, I am led to this/these early memories: _____

_____

_____

_____

5. Who do I become as I bring this part home? How will I now show up in the world? _____

_____

_____

_____

6. I can embrace this new possibility as I imagine it to be so: _____

_____

_____

_____

_____

APPLICATION / DOING THE WORK

1. Name the focus: _____

_____

_____

2. Describe my judgments/reactions: _____

_____

_____

3. This is what I am feeling and what my body is feeling: _____

_____

_____

Now, ask yourself the three questions honestly. (Am I that? Have I ever been that? Do I judge or object to that?) My answer is: _____

_____

_____

4. Bouncing off of the honest answer you gave, ponder this: As I recall this feeling, I am led to this/these early memories: _____

_____

_____

5. Who do I become as I bring this part home? How will I now show up in the world? _____

_____

_____

6. I can embrace this new possibility as I imagine it to be so: _____

_____

_____

_____

_____

1. Name the focus: _____

_____

_____

2. Describe my judgments/reactions: _____

_____

_____

3. This is what I am feeling and what my body is feeling: _____

_____

_____

Now, ask yourself the three questions honestly. (Am I that? Have I ever been that? Do I judge or object to that?) My answer is: _____

_____

_____

4. Bouncing off of the honest answer you gave, ponder this: As I recall this feeling, I am led to this/these early memories: _____

_____

_____

5. Who do I become as I bring this part home? How will I now show up in the world? _____

_____

_____

6. I can embrace this new possibility as I imagine it to be so: _____

_____

_____

_____

1. Name the focus: _____

_____

_____

_____

2. Describe my judgments/reactions: _____

_____

_____

_____

3. This is what I am feeling and what my body is feeling: _____

_____

_____

_____

Now, ask yourself the three questions honestly. (Am I that? Have I ever been that? Do I judge or object to that?) My answer is: _____

_____

_____

_____

4. Bouncing off of the honest answer you gave, ponder this: As I recall this feeling, I am led to this/these early memories: _____

_____

_____

_____

5. Who do I become as I bring this part home? How will I now show up in the world? _____

_____

_____

_____

6. I can embrace this new possibility as I imagine it to be so: _____

_____

_____

_____

_____

1. Name the focus: _____
_____
_____
_____

2. Describe my judgments/reactions: _____
_____
_____
_____

3. This is what I am feeling and what my body is feeling: _____
_____
_____
_____

Now, ask yourself the three questions honestly. (Am I that? Have I ever been that? Do I judge or object to that?) My answer is: _____
_____
_____
_____

4. Bouncing off of the honest answer you gave, ponder this: As I recall this feeling, I am led to this/these early memories: _____
_____
_____
_____

5. Who do I become as I bring this part home? How will I now show up in the world? _____
_____
_____
_____

6. I can embrace this new possibility as I imagine it to be so: _____
_____
_____
_____

1. Name the focus: _____

_____

_____

_____

2. Describe my judgments/reactions: _____

_____

_____

_____

3. This is what I am feeling and what my body is feeling: _____

_____

_____

_____

Now, ask yourself the three questions honestly. (Am I that? Have I ever been that? Do I judge or object to that?) My answer is: _____

_____

_____

_____

4. Bouncing off of the honest answer you gave, ponder this: As I recall this feeling, I am led to this/these early memories: _____

_____

_____

_____

5. Who do I become as I bring this part home? How will I now show up in the world? _____

_____

_____

_____

6. I can embrace this new possibility as I imagine it to be so: _____

_____

_____

_____

_____

Going Directly to Our Emotions: Option 2

Now let's look at our emotions directly and apply the process.

1. Name the feeling and the challenge evoked: _____

_____

_____

_____

_____

Part 2: After asking the three questions honestly (Am I that? Have I ever been that? Do I judge or object to that?), my answer is: _____

_____

_____

_____

_____

_____

_____

2. Set your intention, use a mindshift affirmation and/or a ritual and claim your good as your wholeness, and ask yourself this: Who do I become as I embrace this part of me? _____

_____

_____

_____

_____

_____

_____

3. State your gratitude and claim your good: _____

_____

_____

_____

_____

_____

1. Name the feeling and the challenge evoked: _____

_____

_____

_____

_____

_____

Part 2: After asking the three questions honestly (Am I that? Have I ever been that? Do I judge or object to that?), my answer is: _____

_____

_____

_____

_____

_____

2. Set your intention, use a mindshift affirmation and/or a ritual and claim your good as your wholeness, and ask yourself this: Who do I become as I embrace this part of me? _____

_____

_____

_____

_____

_____

_____

3. State your gratitude and claim your good: _____

_____

_____

_____

_____

_____

_____

1. Name the feeling and the challenge evoked: _____

_____

_____

_____

_____

_____

Part 2: After asking the three questions honestly (Am I that? Have I ever been that? Do I judge or object to that?), my answer is: _____

_____

_____

_____

_____

_____

2. Set your intention, use a mindshift affirmation and/or a ritual and claim your good as your wholeness, and ask yourself this: Who do I become as I embrace this part of me? _____

_____

_____

_____

_____

_____

3. State your gratitude and claim your good: _____

_____

_____

_____

_____

_____

1. Name the feeling and the challenge evoked: _____

_____

_____

_____

_____

_____

Part 2: After asking the three questions honestly (Am I that? Have I ever been that? Do I judge or object to that?), my answer is: _____

_____

_____

_____

_____

_____

2. Set your intention, use a mindshift affirmation and/or a ritual and claim your good as your wholeness, and ask yourself this: Who do I become as I embrace this part of me? _____

_____

_____

_____

_____

_____

3. State your gratitude and claim your good: _____

_____

_____

_____

_____

_____

1. Name the feeling and the challenge evoked: _____

_____

_____

_____

_____

_____

Part 2: After asking the three questions honestly (Am I that? Have I ever been that? Do I judge or object to that?), my answer is: _____

_____

_____

_____

_____

_____

2. Set your intention, use a mindshift affirmation and/or a ritual and claim your good as your wholeness, and ask yourself this: Who do I become as I embrace this part of me? _____

_____

_____

_____

_____

_____

3. State your gratitude and claim your good: _____

_____

_____

_____

_____

_____

1. Name the feeling and the challenge evoked: _____

_____

_____

_____

_____

_____

Part 2: After asking the three questions honestly (Am I that? Have I ever been that? Do I judge or object to that?), my answer is: _____

_____

_____

_____

_____

_____

2. Set your intention, use a mindshift affirmation and/or a ritual and claim your good as your wholeness, and ask yourself this: Who do I become as I embrace this part of me? _____

_____

_____

_____

_____

_____

3. State your gratitude and claim your good: _____

_____

_____

_____

_____

_____

STORY TIME

Meet Missy

Missy spent her entire life feeling left out, unseen, and definitely not welcomed. Within the context of one of my courses, we decided to do some deeper work, and I asked her to share with me the images that came to mind when she wasn't feeling welcomed. The image was of her standing outside a large wall with a large door, but it was closed. She translated this to mean she was not welcome. She translated it that way because it served her self-image and belief system.

Because of the forgiveness and shadow work, she came to realize that she was rejecting herself, that she put herself in that position, and the moment—and this time I mean literally the moment—that we exposed the truth, she realized that she was responsible and that what she believed wasn't true. It had nothing to do with anyone outside of her, especially her family. She knew instantly that not only was she welcome but this was her creation, and she felt freed from this feeling—immediately. The feeling of not belonging transformed instantly, and so did her whole experience.

Maintenance

THIS SECTION OF THE BOOK IS TO SUPPORT YOU GOING FORWARD, BECAUSE THIS IS JUST the beginning.

To stay fresh is to stay in practice.

Here we are returning to the beginning of the book, where I took the time to describe the recommended practices and how they can benefit you with the work. I ponder this question at times: "If I had these practices in my early life, would I have still needed to go through all that pain that it took for me to get here and get free?" I'll never really know, but I do like to shift perspective by pondering these things.

Stay fresh with your practices as laid out here or as you choose to design them. Remember to use the reward system so you continue to rewire your brain and uplift your expectations about your life. Consider having these conversations with others. The more we collectively normalize this subject matter through conversations, the more we spread the word of personal empowerment and freedom throughout your piece of the world.

Shadow work is *not* a one-time thing. This chapter will emphasize the ongoing practices required to stay fresh. There are some movies that you watch over and over again, and there are some books that you return to over time; shadow work requires this same action. Things that give you pleasure call you back to them. While shadow work and the accompanying forgiveness work might not seem pleasurable when you think about them, the rewards are so great that you cannot help but want more of the effect of the work.

This work, when regularly practiced, leaves you forever expanding your awareness toward the wholeness and integration of your whole being.

Theoretically, if you dive into the deepest part of this work and commit to all the practices that you have been taught in this book, you will find yourself freer and stronger than ever before in your life. But there is no guarantee that the need to do the work will stop completely. For this reason, staying fresh with spiritual practices, mindful rituals, and staying aware becomes your job. This is how we keep it fresh, how we keep ourselves fresh.

After decades of forgiveness and shadow work, I have come to the place where I can recognize a potential shadow from a hundred paces. And the time that it now takes me to process this awareness is so fast that it could appear as if I didn't notice something.

STORY TIME

Meet Debbie, the Biker Chick

A student whom we will call Debbie had a bristly kind of neighbor who could sometimes be guilty of not caring about how his behavior and habits of living impacted the people living around him. During one of the times that Debbie was engaging with him, he got a bit fussy and annoyed and placed a trailer on a part of his property that butted up against hers. This restricted some movement and was unsightly. Debbie was pissed off and angry. This feeling activated a shadow in her that she has lovingly come to call Biker Chick.

Debbie has been leery about this side of herself for some time, because it is a rough, tough aspect of her that she is not always proud of, so she has done a lot to hide Biker Chick and deny its existence.

While taking one of my shadow courses, she scheduled a one-on-one with me to take a closer look at this shadow.

Our focus came to her choosing her Biker Chick side, because there was a time in her life when she needed to be strong and to protect herself, so instead of making Biker Chick Debbie wrong, she agreed to thank her and embrace her. Now, it does not always work this fast, but within a couple of days after our work, Debbie went over to this fussy neighbor to ask him to move the trailer, and lo and behold, he seemed to have a whole new attitude. In the next class, I asked her about how it went, and she is now describing this man as nice as pie and easy to get along with. This is spiritual alchemy at its best.

She recognized her shadow, welcomed it home to her wholeness, and this shifted her perspective and how she engaged him. This is what's possible when we go within instead of without.

Recognizing the Golden Shadow, 'Cause It Ain't All Bad!

Energy flows where our attention goes, and where our attention goes, we grow. This is not a new concept, but it comes in quite handy right now. The first stop along our journey caused us to look deep within, to risk some painful memories, and to name the people in our lives who had some influence in the creation of their shadow. We have gone through processing these lists and have learned to accept our shadows rather than avoid them so we could then welcome our disowned parts back home.

Now you begin to reap the benefits over and over again. You have a calm within now that is new, and you get to feel more empowered as you engage the world, because you know that nothing outside of you creates who you are. You live a life by design, and it is beautiful.

But there is more good news. Now you get to take some time getting to know your Golden Shadow. Now that you have learned to stop, breathe, and access your reactions as a learning tool for growth, you have another untapped source for your personal power—the secrets hidden within your Golden Shadow.

HOW DID YOUR GOLDEN SHADOW GET CREATED?

The Golden Shadow gets created because we humans tend to deny our beauty and our strengths, and many of our lighter qualities. We are quick to blame ourselves but slow to take credit for our brilliance. This is a result of the basic shared human trifecta of limitation: I am not worthy, I am not lovable, and I am not enough. These three beliefs have eaten away, just like termites, at the foundation of your being. They serve as a slow and meticulous destroying machine. Then we arrive at adulthood and can barely believe in ourselves. No, this is not everyone, but if you are reading this and know this experience, this is specifically for you.

So, once again, we create our Golden Shadow every time we compliment another person for being a certain way; we project onto them the qualities that we would like to display more of in our life. Now, I am not referring to envying someone for their possessions or being jealous of another person for the life they have, I'm talking about when you look at someone and find yourself wishing that you functioned in the world in a similar fashion.

HOW DOES THE GOLDEN SHADOW DISPLAY ITSELF?

As you walk around engaging in the world, you consistently see the Golden Shadow on people you wish you were. These people are your (s)heroes, and you wish you were more like them or had their talents or their fame. And sometimes this feeling will display as envy.

The Golden Shadow can hide in the people that you compare yourself to. If you are comparing yourself to another, it is because you think they have something that you want or that you don't have. Comparison is never a good practice, but it is a great way for you to recognize where you might be judging yourself and feeling less than.

What kind of person do you see as a role model for you? Do you ever wish you had the life of another? Do you feel cheated or left out? These are great inquiry questions for recognizing your Golden Shadow.

HOW DO I GROW FROM MY GOLDEN SHADOW?

You grow from your Golden Shadow in the same fashion as your dark shadow. You will learn to recognize your potent talents and qualities by seeing them in another, but instead of any resistance to integrating them, we celebrate their existence and look to embrace their evidence within us. Embracing the Golden Shadow involves acknowledging and integrating the positive qualities and potentials that we may have repressed or denied within ourselves.

Golden Shadow Practice

- *Begin with Quiet Contemplation:* Find a quiet and comfortable space where you won't be disturbed. Take a few deep breaths to center yourself.
- *Identify Positive Qualities:* Begin by identifying positive qualities or talents that you've seen in others and maybe you have envied them. These could be creativity, intelligence, leadership skills, kindness, success, or any other positive traits you may have overlooked and believed that you do not possess.

_____

_____

_____

_____

_____

- *Journaling:* Write down the qualities you've identified as you see them in others. Explore how these qualities have shown up in your life, even if you haven't fully embraced them. Remember to answer the question: How does this quality feel in me? _____

_____

_____

_____

_____

- *Imaginary Dialogue:* Close your eyes and visualize a dialogue with your inner child. Imagine talking to a version of yourself that you rejected because of how you once judged yourself. Ask this younger inner child for guidance on how to integrate these traits into your life. _____

_____

_____

_____

_____

_____

- *Affirmations:* Create affirmations that reflect your intention to embrace your Golden Shadow. For example, "I embrace my creativity and let it shine in my life," or "I acknowledge my intelligence and use it for personal growth." _____

_____

_____

_____

_____

- *Use Your Imagination:* Take a few moments to visualize yourself living your life with these qualities fully integrated. See yourself confidently expressing these traits in your daily interactions and activities. _____

_____

_____

_____

_____

_____

- *Take Action:* Choose one small action you can take in the coming days to start cultivating one of these positive qualities. It could be signing up for a class, volunteering, or simply expressing your kindness to someone. _____

_____

_____

_____

_____

_____

- *Gratitude:* End the practice by expressing gratitude for the positive qualities within yourself. Recognize that embracing your Golden Shadow can lead to personal growth and a more fulfilling life. _____

_____

_____

_____

_____

_____

Consistently practicing this exercise can help you embrace and integrate your positive qualities, allowing them to shine and contribute positively to your life and the lives of those around you.

STORY TIME

My New Shero
At one of the forgiveness retreats that I facilitate, this beautiful young woman shared with me that she was feeling guilty for breaking up her nuclear family. When I inquired how that happened, she shared with us that she had decided to tell the truth about sexual abuse that was hidden in her family. Some of her family members could not handle the truth and proceeded to separate themselves.

I listened as she blamed herself and saw that she had been suffering from this choice for years. I paused, I listened to my intuition as to what needed to be said here, and out of my mouth came this: **"YOU are a hero. You stopped the action. You called the perpetrators on the carpet,"** which was something that I had not done in my life. I had been afraid, but she was brave. She is part of my Golden Shadow. And I will now begin to believe in myself and my ability to speak up when the truth needs to be heard.

Mindshifts to Further Your Integration

To read the mindshift scripts in this book is good. To read them regularly is better. To speak them aloud is the most powerful of all. Here is what I would love for you to do for your deepest experience. Almost every smartphone now has a recording app as part of the phone. Take time to record these scripts and play them aloud at night before going to sleep. When you slow down at the end of the night and begin to relax, your brain waves move into a theta state, which is the state of greater receptivity. This is why it is important not to go to sleep upset, if at all possible, because the upset will follow you into your dreams.

Recording the mindshifts provided in this book with your own voice will help you to feel safe and will have a greater impact. On the next few pages, I have provided a few mindshifts to support both your general well-being and for the continued integration of your shadow intentions. Needless to say, add any language you desire, but be sure that it is affirming and optimistic.

Note: You will see me say "I accept this **word**." *Word* is used to indicate the whole mindshift.

MINDSHIFT 1

Off to a Wonderful Sleep

I am a powerful being, filled with love, compassion, intelligence, and all the resources necessary to live a glorious life filled with beauty, joy, and health. I savor the work that I have done and relish the benefits of wholeness.

I choose to think and speak in ways that leave me feeling wonderfully alive and exuberant. As I head to sleep, I affirm my self-worth and declare that I am enough. Affirming this opens me up to greater and greater opportunities. Even as I sleep, I grow. I dream a life of reward and wonder, knowing that I was born with a birthright deserving of good, success, and health.

I accept this word as it deepens faith that I am worthy of all good.

MINDSHIFT 2

I Grow as I Sleep

As I lay my head down to sleep, I do so acknowledging that I am blessed. I am blessed because my life is a holy and beautiful expression of the Universal Intelligence that created all that is. This Universal Intelligence runs through my mind, body, and soul as it causes me to take inventory of my good. Yes, I pause to inventory all of my beauty, my gifts, and my bounty. I am an expression of wholeness in ways I never would have expected. I show up in my life with an open heart, as I am willing to take full responsibility for my life, and in so doing, I am empowered to live an extraordinary life. My sleep and my dreams reward me with a sense of grace, calm, and peace. My dreams are now a reflection of this truth. Each night, I let go and allow my consciousness to gift me with dreams of inspiration.

All is well and with a bounty of gratitude, I release this word into the Universal Intelligence.

MINDSHIFT 3

Expanding My Life

I begin by getting mindful, and becoming aware of my breath. With every breath I take, I am moved toward a sweet and gentle calm, and I take this calm into my sleep. Yes, as I ready myself to sleep, I surrender all struggle, worry, and concern, and my load is made light. As I seek to be whole, I do so because I know that I am surrounded by love. Love that lifts and inspires me every moment of my day.

I affirm that everything I need to expand my life exists within my consciousness. As my consciousness grows and my awareness expands, I move to a greater state of wholeness. Alive within me is all the intelligence, understanding, and strength required to be the free individual I care to be. This is made possible because I let go of all my self-judgment and accept myself exactly as I am and as I am not.

Every day, I am more skilled at recognizing my disowned parts, and with each part that I see and engage, I am empowered to love it and call it back home. Each time I do this, I move into greater wholeness.

I am stronger than I ever imagined, more powerful than I thought possible, and I am ready for the full integration of my shadow. As I become whole, there is a love that exudes from me that alters my life permanently and touches the lives of the people I care about in the most wonderful way possible. Yes, I am made whole again, and it is a glorious experience.

I now call my shadow parts back home. I cease needing to project them onto others, and this empowers me to stand strong, tall, and extremely happy, for I am made whole from my efforts. I call all this good, and I release this mindshift to demonstrate in me and as me immediately.

Your Lineage Is Your Legacy

Healing your shadow holds immense significance when it comes to your legacy. Your legacy is not just about the material or tangible assets you pass on to future generations; it's also about the impact you've had on the people around you, the values you've embodied, and the lessons you've taught. Here's why healing our shadow is crucial in shaping a positive and lasting legacy:

- First and foremost, shadow work helps you break the cycle of generational patterns and unhealed wounds. Many of our shadow aspects are influenced by the unresolved issues and emotional baggage passed down through our family history. By addressing and healing these aspects, you prevent the perpetuation of negative patterns, thus creating a more harmonious and healthy family legacy.

- Furthermore, shadow work leads to greater self-awareness and emotional intelligence in general. When you delve into your shadow, you are better equipped to understand your triggers and reactions. This heightened self-awareness allows you to make conscious choices and decisions that are aligned with your true values, thereby setting a positive example for others to follow. Your ability to manage and navigate your emotions and relationships more effectively can be a key part of your legacy, teaching future generations the importance of empathy, resilience, and self-improvement.

- Lastly, a healed shadow allows you to live a more authentic and purpose-ful life. This authenticity is magnetic and inspiring to others. By embracing your imperfections and showing the courage to work on them, you demonstrate that personal growth and self-discovery are lifelong journeys. The message of your healed YOU will be woven into your legacy and can inspire those who come after you to embark on their own paths of self-improvement, and thereby contribute positively to the world. In essence, healing your shadow influences your legacy by breaking destructive cycles, fostering emotional intelligence, and inspiring others to live more authentic and fulfilling lives.

Your lineage, that which was handed down to you either within your lifetime or through ancestral memories and DNA, is your legacy as is, but only if you don't heal the pain. When you invest time and energy into healing the impact from your lineage, then as a change agent, you get to break the chain of pain and have your legacy not be one of unchecked pain and suffering but one of heal-ing, love, and wholeness. A whole you creates a healthier legacy.

When you find yourself at a crossroads with someone you love, especially a family member, stop and ask yourself these questions before you give free rein to your mouth.

Ask:

How will this decision and my behavior impact those I care about? _____
_____
_____

How will my legacy be impacted if I do not question what is happening now? ___
_____
_____

How can I stand for love in my family? _____
_____

How can I love and accept my family instead of judging them and making them wrong? _____
_____

How would I like to be an influence in my family, as my legacy? _____
_____
_____

How would I like to be remembered in my family? _____
_____

This helps return your focus to the intention that you set early in the work. You are doing this work for a reason. Sure, part of that reason might be for others, but in the end, you must do it for you and your internal landscape, because that is where the seeds of growth will spring forth from.

Revisit your why and your intention. Take time to print out these two things, leave them where you will see them regularly, and return to them regularly.

Count your blessings—yes, really. Don't ignore this piece of advice because it is common like a silly saying on a Hallmark card. Counting your blessings and having a gratitude practice are two of the most surefire ways to uplift yourself and to shift and reframe your perspective. As we already know, when we see differently and direct our attention toward our desired outcome, shift happens. When we are clear of our direction, that which is in the way is moved out of the way and our path becomes more obvious to us.

Quick practice: List ten aspects of your life for which you are grateful. Remember to be grateful for your courage to do the work.

_____

_____

_____

_____

_____

_____

_____

_____

_____

_____

IF MORE PEOPLE TOOK OWNERSHIP OF THEIR SHADOW, THERE WOULD BE A LOT LESS VIOLENCE IN THE WORLD.

Think about it: To struggle, another must be involved. We struggled because, before now, we believed that some aspects of the world were against us. Well, begin to imagine differently. Imagine a world where we own our responses, blame no one outside ourselves, and practice forgiveness along with our shadow work. We would be less distracted by appearances and more focused on being a healing element.

Create a bold statement of who you are and how you would like your legacy to appear.

Example: *I choose to be a whole, loving, and forgiving influence in my family because I am powerful.*

Now, your turn:

_____

_____

MINDSHIFT

Being a Change Agent

As I enter the path to recognize and heal my shadow, I am more empowered with each shadow that I choose to love, embrace, and accept. This causes me to integrate my shadow and to move toward wholeness. From that place of ever-increasing wholeness I become a change agent within my family. I acknowledge the history and the pain of my family. I acknowledge where there might have been suffering. I acknowledge that every family member did the best they could even when their best might have been unskilled.

As I embrace my shadow and choose to love all the influences of my family instead of judging them, I become part of the solution in the greatest conceivable way. I break the chain of pain in my family, blessing my lineage and blessing my legacy. All those who follow me will have a path of love, acceptance, and generosity to walk upon. This is who I choose to be in the world.

Feeling greatly empowered, I release the spoken word to my inner intelligence governed by Universal Intelligence, and I simply become the intention of my word. And so it is.

Habits for Maintenance

Healing the shadow, a process rooted in self-awareness and self-acceptance, involves consistent inner work. Here's a list of weekly and daily habits to help you address and heal your shadow:

Weekly Habits

1. **JOURNALING:** Dedicate time each week to journal your thoughts, emotions, and experiences. Reflect on any recurring patterns or unresolved issues that arise.
2. **THERAPY OR COUNSELING:** If possible, attend regular therapy or counseling sessions with a trained professional who can guide you through shadow work if you are feeling tender.
3. **MINDFULNESS MEDITATION:** Practice mindfulness meditation to become more aware of your thoughts and emotions without judgment. This can help you identify and work through shadow aspects.
4. **READING AND LEARNING:** Read books and articles or watch videos on psychology, self-development, and shadow work to deepen your understanding of the process.
5. **SELF-REFLECTION:** Set aside time for self-reflection, perhaps through guided exercises or prompts, to explore your past experiences and their impact on your current behaviors.

Daily Habits

1. **SELF-COMPASSION:** Start your day with self-compassion. Speak to yourself kindly and remind yourself that you are on a journey of growth and healing.
2. **MINDFUL AWARENESS:** Throughout the day, practice being present and mindful of your thoughts, feelings, and reactions, especially in triggering situations.

3. **EMOTIONAL PROCESSING:** Take time to acknowledge and process your emotions. Don't suppress or judge them; instead, allow yourself to feel and express them constructively.

4. **SHADOW JOURNAL:** Maintain a "shadow journal" where you document any specific shadow aspects, triggers, or insights that arise on a daily basis.

5. **MEDITATIVE PRACTICES:** Incorporate meditative practices like breathwork, body scanning, or visualizations to explore your inner landscape and bring shadow aspects to light.

6. **SELF-INQUIRY:** Ask yourself questions like "Why do I feel this way?" or "What past experiences might be influencing this reaction?" regularly to delve deeper into your subconscious.

7. **HEALTHY BOUNDARIES:** Practice setting and maintaining healthy boundaries in your relationships, ensuring that you don't overextend yourself or tolerate mistreatment.

8. **FORGIVENESS:** Work on forgiving yourself and others for past hurts and mistakes. This can be a powerful tool for shadow healing.

9. **SEEK FEEDBACK:** Encourage open and honest feedback from trusted friends or loved ones to gain external perspectives on your blind spots.

10. **CREATIVITY AND EXPRESSION:** Engage in creative outlets like art, writing, or music to give voice to your inner world and explore your subconscious.

Remember that shadow work is a lifelong process, and it's essential to approach it with patience and self-compassion. These habits can help you gradually heal and integrate your shadow aspects, leading to greater self-awareness and personal growth.

STORY TIME

Meet Sharon

Sharon began taking classes to heal a particular relationship she had with someone within her congregation. Her relationship with this individual was contemptuous at best. While they had a love for each other, their styles of functioning in the ministry and in life were completely divergent, although they needed to be able to collaborate.

Both Sharon and this other individual started their journey with my Forgiveness Course and then continued on to the Shadow Course.

Working diligently on herself, Sharon tracked her shadow, her reactions, and kept asking the three questions: Am I that, have I ever been that, or do I judge or object to that? This led to massive truths being exposed. She learned to set up a healthy boundary for herself, did her forgiveness and shadow work, and reported that her entire ministry began to take a different form. She was thrilled. As for that relationship, well, that was part of the boundary, but it was implemented with love and compassion.

She changed focus from the work being an outside challenge to accepting and loving the shadow, stopped being distracted by the outside world, did the healing work, and her world changed accordingly. The work works if you work it.

A Simplified Version of the Process

Begin with now. We begin by assessing our lives and our reactions. Your reactions and triggers are a gift. They point the way. No, they do not feel good. Your discomfort will try to distract you; therefore, discipline and dedication to the process are required. Without discipline you will feel convinced that your pain, while it resides within, is caused by another—it is not. (There is no other. There is no outside.)

Follow the feeling. We name our feeling reaction, knowing that it was birthed in a much earlier version of ourselves. Once named, we use this feel like an energetic cord: Follow it slowly and allow it to lead us to the root of the root.

Bless and thank the moment. We express gratitude right in the face of the feeling, the story, and our reaction. We do this because we have prepared ourselves through our training to know that all this pain serves as a distraction to our wholeness. As we bless the feeling, the blessing begins to transform the experience—it has an alchemical effect.

Get grounded and settled. By the mindfulness practices that you implement, you will settle your body, quiet your reactions, arrest the fear, and choose your next steps wisely.

Apply mindshift. As you have learned in this material, the storehouse for our stories and pain is within our subconscious. Every time we are stimulated, we are offered an opportunity to reintegrate a feeling within. We then use mindshift prayer/treatment to support our process.

Rebalance and restore. Although we do all of our healing work within our own mind, heart, and consciousness, there are times that—after much soul searching and contemplation—we might be inspired to act. It might be as simple as performing a ritual, doing some journaling, writing a letter, or making a phone call—or any act of self-care that supports your healing.

Mindshift Explained

Any explanation about mindshift affirmative prayer used in this material is explained from a spiritual and metaphysical point of view, as taught in the Centers for Spiritual Living worldwide generated by their founder, Ernest Holmes, and his ultimate work: *The Science of Mind*.

Spiritual Mind Treatment (Mindshift) is an art and science that individuals study and refine for years. But even a rudimentary understanding and application of it will benefit you.

For our purpose here, we will describe mindshift as having five steps. Please know that this is being presented in a purposefully simplistic manner.

Here are the steps to a basic mindshift affirmation. After the steps there is a sample provided for you.

1. **RECOGNITION:** Recognition is where we describe through language our understanding of God/Spirit/Life. We describe it in order to create the feeling experience within us. When we treat/pray/mindshift, we always speak language that assumes our oneness with this sacred essence.

   Example with the word God: There is only One. It is a beautiful Intelligence that exists everywhere, avails Itself to everyone equally and is felt throughout. This One shows up to me, through me and as me. I call this One God.

   Example without the word God: There is only One. One Power, One Presence, One Love that avails Itself in, through, and as me easily, immediately, always.

2. **UNIFICATION:** Unification is the step where I declare that the God/Spirit/Life that I have just described and I are one. Unification is the acknowledgment that God by any name exists right where we are without exception. So, whether you relate to and align yourself with a God or an Intelligence, what matters here is that you recognize that this One lives and demonstrates *as* you. (This is critical to mindshift affirmation.)

3. **DEMONSTRATION/MANIFESTATION/DESIRED OUTCOME:** This is the step where you give language to your desired outcome. Here, the language must be extremely affirmative, always stated in the *now*, using descriptive language that will engage your imagination, your faith, and your feeling senses.

4. **GRATITUDE:** This step is where you either connect with or begin to cultivate faith that your desired outcome is guaranteed. This step is where you give language to your gratitude for the outcome—assuming the satisfaction of your outcome. We state our gratitude in advance because we believe that any word spoken is acted upon by God/Intelligence/Spirit/Life and that which is claimed/declared must manifest.

5. **RELEASE:** The release step is the next step of faith. The release step basically says this: I believe that that which I have spoken is acted upon and demonstrated by the Power that dwells within me. I faithfully release this mindshift to the Law of Life (or the Universe, my Higher Power, etc.). And so it is!

Spiritually, when I use the word "Law" above, what I mean is that power that takes our spoken word, acts upon it, and delivers it to the Faithful. The Law, however, can only work for you, on your behalf to the level of your faith, conviction, and willingness. This means that those who speak their word and release their word faithfully increase their odds of receiving their desired outcome. If doubt or fear enter the mind of the one seeking to shift their thoughts, doubt and fear become new active powers of demonstration and will negate and erase that which has been spoken. For example: Gardeners plant their seeds, and they care for the seeds, but they *never* dig them up to see if they are sprouting. They must trust, they must have faith, or they will interrupt the growing. The same applies when you set an intention for change.

If one struggles with faith and/or a belief in this Law as a power in their life, then that individual should begin by mindshifting to increase his/her faith, not in God but of God or whatever Universal Power they subscribe to.

MINDSHIFT

Increasing Faith and Surrender

STEP 1: *There is a power and a presence that is everywhere present; it is potent, beautiful, alive, and vibrant. I call this One—God/Spirit/Life/ Intelligence. There is only One, and I recognize this power as a Power for good and for transformation.*

STEP 2: *This One that I call God lives and breathes in, through, and as me. It exists at the core of my being, and It empowers within me all transformation.*

STEP 3: *As I surrender to this One and allow it to empower me, I am free from the effects of my shadow, yes, I am free, I am free, I am free. That which has been hovering in me and living within my subconscious no longer has influence within my life. Any aspects of any shadows that have taken residence within my subconscious, that have been in any way informing my behavior or my decisions are now made inviable, ineffective, and no longer have any influence within my life. I declare that there is only One Power and Source in my life, and as I identify with this One, I rise up, freeing myself to be bold, to be creative, to be healthy and prosperous. As I shed my shadow, I am lighter than ever before, free to see life from a whole new perspective, free to venture out into the world as perfect, whole, and complete. I am more alive now than I have been for years. I feel a new creative energy surging through my mind, my heart, and my body temple. I am delivered. I am free.*

STEP 4: *With a bounty of gratitude and sweet expectancy, I express my gratitude with my words and my feeling tone.*

STEP 5: *Faithfully and with full conviction, I release this word to the Law, to Love, and to the Awe of Life. And so it is!*

Be a Loving Spiritual Warrior

To be a spiritual warrior with the ability to influence change, ask yourself this: Do I want to be right, or do I want to be happy?

Let us take this in another direction. Are you willing to take a stand for Love, of Love, with Love for your greatest "enemy"? Can you choose *to be* Love so ultimately that your Love of another becomes more important than what they did to you or intended to do, how they got over you, and how you were hurt?

What if letting go of the hurt *freed* you completely? Could you? Would you?

Can you love someone more than they can love themselves? Can you love someone past their history and bad decisions? Can you *be Love* without needing to be right or to prove your superiority?

Follow me here now for a moment. Let us come away from any assessment, of any kind, having to do with another. Let me ask you these questions again. Can you love yourself more than ever before? Can you love yourself past your history and bad decisions? Can you *be Love* without needing to be right or to prove your superiority? Can you relax *into Love*? The way you love forms your legacy.

Imagine walking in a state of Love that emanated from deep within your being. *Imagine* and integrate into who you are with full awareness of this state. Imagine your ex, without needing them to be different, and then choose to love them. Imagine your boss fired you without merit, and whenever you think of her, you are free to *be* in a state of Love. Imagine moving beyond rejection of your mom, dad, or any siblings and just again choose to love them *even* if you don't like or approve of their behavior.

Remember while self-love, forgiveness, and shadow work lead you to your whole self, it continues to be wise to set boundaries so you feel safe. Boundaries are an act of self-love. They keep you safe and keep you from engaging in a relationship that causes you discomfort. And at any point you get to update or change the boundaries as you see fit. If the nature of your relationship changes, then you can alter the boundary.

The kind of Love of which I speak here has nothing to do with approval or rejection. It is, however, about emanating the vibration of Love so definitely that no one can hang their objections on you.

Might you have to let go of some things—YEP!
Will you have to forgive behavior—YEP!
Will you suffer because you let go and chose to love instead—NOPE!
Will you look like a fool for letting go and loving anyway—MAYBE!
BUT WHO CARES WHEN THE REWARD BECOMES GLORI-OUSLY, FULLY EXPRESSED AS YOU!

Coping Mechanisms

Sometimes we need a way to handle all those emotions that we are unearthing but in a healthy way. The following suggestions will help you process your emotions while practicing good self-care. Remember these rituals cannot replace all the deep and meaningful work that is required. Use them in addition to, not instead of that work.

Buy a teddy!

Yes, corny in so many ways, but because love lives at the foundation of all this work, I suggest love in a fun and demonstratable way. Buy yourself a stuffed animal or baby doll. Buy one that really makes you want to hug it. Buy a high-quality stuffed animal that satisfies you kinesthetically. It is particularly important that you want to touch it because this is the game plan.

When you are feeling a bit tender and need some touch, hold your bear with great care. If you are sad and feeling down, hold and comfort the bear as if it were your inner child. If you have just processed something big, consider talking to this bear that you have named and tell it how happy you are that your shadow parts have returned to be part of your whole again. Listen to yourself and all that comes out of your mouth. When we allow ourselves to talk out loud, sometimes we surprise ourselves with what we say. This is how we continue to grow our self-awareness.

Imagine starting the conversation like this: "Hey there, Cuddles, how are you today? I was having a rough day today and couldn't wait to come home and tell you about my day and cuddle with you." When you're talking to your teddy bear, speak about yourself in kind, loving ways; talk to that inner child in you.

Potential rituals

Rote rituals, where your emotions are not fully invested, will only supply a temporary feel-good relief, if any. However, when you set an intention, surround that intention with a ritual, and feel the presence in the moment, then you can have a profound experience. I personally enjoy a well-developed ritual that has been created with conscious intent and purpose. When I use rituals in conjunction with a high intent, I experience major shifts in my life. I have personally received help from letter writing, releasing rituals, and the creating of altars that serve as a reminder in my home to stay aware.

But here are some other rituals and practices that have brought change to my life. I have climbed to the top of a pyramid in Mexico to participate in a ritual to marry my higher power, I have fasted to get in touch with my truest desires, I have fasted from all judgment and gossip for extended periods of time, I have attended and organized my own silent retreats, for which I have written a book, and I have walked on fire. The last ritual afforded me the realization that fear is a choice, which is a concept that I needed to get on top of.

A Few Simple Suggestions

- Write a letter to your shadow and thank it for guiding you to wholeness. Then you can keep it in a sacred place, maybe stuffed in a book that you often turn to.

- Create a releasing ritual. On a piece of paper, write the aspects of your life that you are committing to change. Even though you are letting go of something, still form it in an affirming way. For example: *I now release all my self-judgment so I may be free.* Then burn it ritualistically.

- Engage Mother Nature. Go for a walk while carrying some flower seeds, and throughout your walk, just drop the seeds and let Mother

Nature grow them or not. Once released, they are no longer under your care.

- Buy a candle and dedicate this candle to your wholeness. Place it somewhere in your home that is safe but that you can see daily. (Stay safe.) When you come home at night, light the candle as a testament to your wholeness.

- Choose a touchstone to use as a reminder. Choose a stone, a gem, a coin, or something small that you can carry on your person or keep with you in your bag. Sit in silence and speak your intentions for your personal freedom into the chosen item. Then just keep it around and touch it throughout your day as a reminder of your wholeness.

Be a Champion for Someone

Once you start to notice improvements and relish the fruits of your efforts, share the happiness and insights you've gained. Do this not by trying to fix others, but by showing love, extending support, and affirming their worth. Look beyond their external demeanor to understand their struggles, and most importantly, be your authentic self. Begin to look people directly in their eye with the intent of recognizing their perfection.

Practicing non-judgment enhances your approachability, especially around children and grandchildren, and don't be surprised if you begin to deepen your relationship to animals. Be a positive and wholesome presence now that you've learned not to take things personally and to see the inner beauty in both yourself and others.

The more you share your happiness and personal growth, the more these qualities flourish within you. *People will recognize a change in you, and when they inquire, explain how accepting yourself, both your strengths and flaws, has been transformative.* Share your journey with them. Remind your loved ones that they, too, are worthy of self-love without conditions.

Every time you stand up for yourself or others, your strength and determination are bolstered.

The Language of Co-creation

As you have begun to understand and heal your shadow, your listening will become more fine-tuned, both to what you hear yourself say and to others around you. It will become easier to spot the habits of non-responsibility and projection of the shadow. As we become more practiced, our language will follow suit. This chart supplies some practice.

UNPRACTICED PEOPLE SAY:	PRACTICED PEOPLE SAY:
He/she made me angry.	I feel angry.
I'll get back at him/her.	I choose not to give my power away.
He/she is a liar and should be punished.	This behavior sparks something in me that I must heal.
This is all your fault.	I take responsibility for what I am feeling.
It's all happening outside.	It's all happening inside.
They are just jealous of me.	I am willing to be present and see others.
It's not my fault.	
They are all against me.	
It's not me.	
They always do that.	
I have no say in the matter.	

Why is this happening to me?	
If only they wouldn't do that.	
If they hadn't said that I wouldn't feel this way.	
I'm not a racist.	

See the examples above where both sides are filled in, then on the right side, where there are blanks, complete them with your renewed understanding. Then, while being radically honest, put a little check mark next to anything that you have heard yourself say. Put two check marks if you have heard yourself say them often, and pay attention going forward, either doing more shadow work, forgiveness work, or change your language to create new habits.

Intrinsic Rewards

JOY—

If you are reading this, you have done the work, you have looked within, and you have set intentions and a new direction for your life. By now some meaningful things have shifted within, and you are seeing the world differently.

When you dedicate yourself to the kind of transformative work discussed in this book, you'll discover not only the gifts and changes highlighted but also some subtle yet profound rewards that will stay with you for life.

One of the most wonderful of these rewards is *joy*. Joy emerges as a natural, subtle reward after navigating through the necessary emotional work and confronting your inner shadows. Once these shadows no longer obscure your view, you reclaim your inherent right to joy. Joy is not a goal to be achieved; it's a spiritual element woven into the very fabric of your being, an intrinsic part of who you are. Your inner emotional landscape will now produce the most beautiful of fruits for your labor.

Your efforts to awaken and become more conscious will remind you that you deserve this joy. Each person who strives for personal growth and elevation contributes to a healthier humanity. Your wholeness enriches all of us, for when you are complete, you become a blessing to humanity.

In this state, you are a reward to yourself, and you'll often be amazed by the beauty you can now fully appreciate. Simple joys like sunsets, sunrises, the blooming of spring flowers, or the laughter of a baby will ignite within you a sense of joy and awe, as you are no longer preoccupied with life's dramas.

Take a moment to list the people in your life that you love and would love to influence—again, not with any force but with an abundance of love and compassion.

Make your list here: _____

_____

_____

_____

_____

_____

_____

_____

_____

_____

In Closing

BY NOW, YOU HAVE GOTTEN TO KNOW SOME THINGS ABOUT MY LIFE. I SHARE THE UGLY because I no longer want to hide or protect it. My freedom comes from telling my story to inspire others to be free. My hope is to continue to do the work fiercely and constantly so I can meet you in the field of possibility as you discover your true essence.

My dream for humanity at large is peace, but with the population of the planet being over eight billion, I will settle for spreading the word as far and as wide as I can. I am here, as are others, to educate as many people as possible to love and forgive themselves and to love their full essence. Let us move into our wholeness, reach out our hand to another, and lift them up.

May your journey be paved with peace, love, and compassion.

May you model the process for others to follow.

May you live a life filled with joy, forever embracing more freedom.

May you love yourself as you are and as you are not like never before.

And may you consider gifting a copy of this book to those you love, and be in deep and intimate conversations that expand your love as you share. Sharing is caring.

You are seen, loved, and appreciated, and you are a valuable part of a healthy society—welcome.

Many blessings,
Michelle

Mindshifts Throughout the Book

References

Psychology and Alchemy by Carl Jung

Atlas of the Heart by Brené Brown

The Four Agreements by Don Miguel Ruiz

The Dark Side of the Light Chasers by Debbie Ford

The Shadow Effect by Deepak Chopra, Debbie Ford, and Marianne Williamson

The Myth of Normal by Gabor Maté, MD, with Daniel Maté

The Body Keeps the Score: Brain, Mind, and Body in the Healing of Trauma by Bessel van der Kolk, MD

It's the Thought That Counts by David Hamilton, PhD

How God Changes Your Brain by Andrew Newberg, MD, and Mark Robert Waldman

Radical Forgiveness by Colin Tipping

Forgiveness: A Path, a Promise, a Way of Life by Michelle Wadleigh

The Science of Mind by Ernest Holmes

The Prophet by Kahlil Gibran

The Quantum Doctor by Amit Goswami, PhD

Original Blessing: A Primer in Creation Spirituality Presented in Four Paths, Twenty-Six Themes, and Two Questions by Matthew Fox

Whole Brain Living by Jill Bolte Taylor, PhD

The Big Leap by Gay Hendricks

May Silence Be Your Guide by Michelle Wadleigh

Acknowledgments

Thank you to my husband for all of his support, Veda King Blanchard for her sharp eye and interest in this project, all of my students for allowing me learn from them and enriching this material, and a special thank you to Joel Fotinos both for his encouragement and for demanding more of me. And thank you to my friends Gesa Nichols, Jo Christiana, and Jim Starke for their relentless support.

And as always, I must invoke the name of my Spiritual Teacher, Reverend Dr. Rita Sperling-Rogers: Without her, I wouldn't be me.

Index

INDEX

inquiry, 38, 47, 65, 154
  contemplation and, 4, 18,
    20, 120
  defined, 9, 20
  Golden Shadow questions,
    199
  with inventory support,
    132–36
  radical honesty and, 20, 120
  self-, 150, 211
  steps for shadow, 177–81
insecurity, 32, 34, 50, 96,
    155, 180
  with addicted to being
    liked, 125
  as emotional trigger, 28,
    151
  inner child and, 81–82
  projection and, 122–23
integration
  through emotions directly,
    153
  healing and, 151
  MAPs to further, 202–5
  of rejected parts, 56,
    143–46
  through relationships,
    152–53
intention
  with emotional intensity, 3
  mindful, 161
  of non-judgment as
    spiritual practice, 18n1
  pre-work, 95
  shadow work, 100–101, 120
inventory
  MAP for taking, 121–22
  radical honesty and taking,
    120
  reward for doing, 141
  shadow list, 128–31,
    174–75
  support, 132–36

inward, MAP for looking, 76
It's the Thought That Counts
  (Hamilton), 22

jealousy, 27, 110, 128, 180,
    198
  confusing other emotions
    with, 90
  as emotional trigger, 28,
    151
  inner child work and, 72
journaling
  denying yourself to be
    liked, 126–27
  emotions, 98–99, 110–11
  Golden Shadow practice,
    199–200
  gratefulness, 208
  growth, 170
  to inner self, 84
  integrating whole self, 145
  legacy, 207, 209
  letter writing, 18, 26–27,
    59–60, 73–74, 77–78, 80,
    84, 164, 219
  parenting and thanking
    children, 69
  parenting thoughts and
    reactions, 64
  personality types, 133–34
  prioritizing others first,
    124, 127
  releasing ritual, 220
  returning to wholeness,
    179
  reward system, 52, 53, 54
  rewiring brain with, 49–50,
    52–54
  self-assessment, 137–39
  self-compassion, 171
  shadow, 211
  shadow inventory list,
    128–31, 174–75

shadow work intentions,
    100–101
  in shadow work tool kit,
    18, 23
  thank you shadow, 77–78,
    162–64
  triggers and reactions, 121
  as weekly maintenance
    habit, 210
  why do shadow work,
    103–4
joy, 223
judgment, 37–38, 81–82, 150.
    See also self-judgment
  non-, 17–19, 18n1, 33–35,
    97
  repressed emotions and,
    89–90
Jung, Carl, 31, 78

Knowing yourself. *See*
  self-knowledge

language (words). *See also*
  Mindshifting Affirmative
  Prayer
  affirmative, 16–17, 22
  of co-creation, 221–22
  complaining, 81, 95, 97,
    103, 106, 128
  dialogue, 45, 200, 218–19
  for emotions, 90–91
  gossip, 35, 81, 95, 97–98,
    113, 128, 219
  mind, body and, 21–22
  self-talk, 79, 136, 218–19
laughing, 33, 75, 80
law, 9, 76
  of creation, 10, 85, 116
  with spoken word, 149,
    215, 216
learning, reading and,
    210

About the Author

Lee Seidenberg

REVEREND DR. MICHELLE WADLEIGH is a coach, teacher, speaker, workshop and retreat facilitator, and minister. Her preferred pronouns are she and her and her favorite title today is "Nana." Michelle is the co-founder and director of the Planned Happiness Institute and the PHI Coaching Academy. After decades of metaphysical study, Michelle founded the Center for Spiritual Living North Jersey, where she served as spiritual leader and pastor for twenty-two years.

She was born in Jersey City, New Jersey, and was raised in Hudson County: a proud Jersey girl all the way. She is passionate about this work but is always willing to learn something new and can be found laughing at herself often and out loud.

Michelle can be heard as a guest on many podcasts or found offering a keynote address. Michelle has spent years developing her courses in forgiveness and shadow work and perfecting her unique approach to working with individuals called the Radical Release Method. Michelle is the author of several books: *Forgiveness: A Path, a Promise, a Way of Life; Prosperous Me; 40 Days to Freedom: A Lenten Practice for the Modern Mind;* and *May Silence Be Your Guide.*